THE DIGITAL VILLAIN

Notes on the Numerology,
Parapsychology,
and
Metaphysics
of the Computer

ROBERT M. BAER, University of California, Berkeley

Poli contra ventum urinara

ADDISON-WESLEY PUBLISHING
Reading, Massachusetts
Menlo Park, California · London ·

D0824908

The book is published
under the editorship of
Michael A. Harrison

Preface

Those who frequently use computers tend to become habituated—sometimes addicted—to them. The reason is easy to understand: the ease with which we access the enormous capability of these machines and pleasure in the performance which they so readily yield. As in the case of addicts generally, we tend not to analyze critically the source of our pleasure. (As the diabolic character says in *Giles Goat-Boy*: "Never mind the question. The Answer's power!") But this book is partially concerned with the question. We admit that the computer is not simply a magical genie whose awesome might may be summoned up merely by polishing an old deck of IBM cards. In the beginning the computer was invented to solve the problem. What seems to have happened is that the computer has *become* the problem. So now the question is, what can we invent to...

We have explored the question in an introductory computer science course given at Berkeley for the past several years. In doing so, it seemed fruitful to apply a dichotomy to the course: devoting one part to the *idea* of the computer and one part to programming a particular computer. It is with the first part that these Notes are concerned, and programming details do not intervene here except in some minor and innocuous ways.

Berkeley, California   R.M.B.
January 1972

Contents

Part I A View From Within: the golden bit

Prologue

Whereas the development of technology is advancing at an unparalleled rate of speed and is rapidly coming to affect every level of American life; and whereas the operations of industry and Government are coming more and more to rely on highly sophisticated computer technology . . .

And whereas Congress needs a committee ready and able to evaluate the effects of technology on the operations of Government, on the democratic institutions and processes basic to the United States, and on the basic human and civil rights on our citizens:

Now, therefore, be it *resolved*,

That there is hereby created a select committee to . . . conduct a full and complete investigation and study of the development and proliferation of technology . . . including the role and effectiveness of computer technology in the operations of industry and Government, the consequences of using computers to solve social questions which traditionally have been addressed without the assistance of computers . . .

The committee shall also study the use of computers . . . in gathering and centralizing information on individuals and the effect of such activity on the human and civil rights . . .

House Resolution 717
91st Congress
November 19, 1969

Man, although a spontaneous, unpredictable, free-willed creature, is fascinated by the mechanical. The child mimics marionettes. Adults upon the parade ground zealously simulate automata in motion. The technology of mechanism structures society and prosthetizes the individual: Man has invented machines to do his writing, his listening, his talking, his running, his flying, his orbiting. The ultimate technological development is the computer—to do his thinking.

The computer is a most remarkable instrument. Silent, motionless, reliable. Able to effect almost endless chains of instructions with precision and dispatch, requiring only that the monologues of command pitched against it be phrased with a modest degree of syntactic exactness. Able to respond instantly to human or mechanical direction—or to react with assigned delay to stored dictation. An instrument—purely mechanical—which mirrors man's intellectual exercises, plays his intellectual games, controls his satellites and space vehicles, monitors his chemical factories and his coronary care units, and teaches his children arithmetic and language.

The computer is the most beautiful and useful of man's inventions. The manufacturers' brochures say so.

And one might wonder: Does anyone say nay? (There are, as Marat said, always some who doubt.) But skeptical assessments are hard to come by. We have collected a few of these in Part II of this book. Literature is concerned with the contradictions of man's condition. Theatre is concerned with the more dramatic of these contradictions. The views collected in Part II are drawn mostly from literature and the theatre: They reflect upon the paradox of man's relation to the mechanical and some subtleties in the relation of the computer to man. They express, for the most part, a common theme. It need not be stated. We all know it already.

But first things first. Part I is meant to provide a casual sketch of the computer as seen from the inside—the when and where of its coming, some aspects of its fabrication and capability, a brusque review of the commercial gambits it has generated on the Big Board and the gyrations of the industrial—and academic—segments of the establishment upon the event of its incursion. In short, what we do with it and what it does with us. (Part II, on the other hand, is a view from the outside.)

There are many areas of relevance which we do not consider here. Some of these are particularly fascinating. For example, where small clutches of computers are linked together to form an organizational whole, we find an invariant pecking order: One or more smaller, less capable machines are given administrative authority which they wield over the faster, more highly structured and valuable machines. Is this mirroring of the familiar structure of many educational and commercial establishments an accidental irony, or an unsurprising embodiment of some Parkinsonian law of organizational evolution? Of course, we rely upon the anthropology of computers to supply the answer, yet the highest councils of science have implied, with studied indirection, that this is a darker area of research, better left unprobed. And what of the population of computers, taken all together? By virtue of their prevalence and power, and the driving rate of increase of their numbers, we may soon be forced to recognize them as a substantial part of our society—the Fourth World—and so be compelled to deal more attentively with the social, legal, and moral problems which they pose.

For the most part these questions are not addressed in this book. We tread more familiar terrain. To reveal the depth and substance of the territory we depend throughout upon the references. But do not expect these to point the optimal path—for the most part they simply indicate that someone has passed this way before.

1   The Semantics of Computer Science

"When I use a word," Humpty Dumpty said, in rather a scornful tone, "it means just what I choose it to mean—neither more nor less."

"The question is," said Alice, "whether you *can* make words mean so many different things."

"The question is," said Humpty Dumpty, "which is to be master—that's all."

Lewis Carroll

... "computers" means "living computers"—the hardware, their programs or algorithms, and all that goes with them. Computer science is the study of the phenomena surrounding computers.

Newell, Perlis, and Simon
Science 157 (1967), 1373–4

.   .   .   .

If there is such a thing as Computer Science, what is it? It is, of course, whatever the computing establishment says it is. The establishment itself consists of the ivory tower residents (the university computer science departments), the Gold Coast residents (the captains of the computer industry), and the professional societies. Some of the societies are:

British Computer Society

The Canadian Information Processing Society

Association Française pour la Cybernetique, Economique et Technique

Indian Society for Automation and Information Sciences
Associzione Italiano per il Calcolo Automatico
Svenska Samfundet for Informations Behandlung

(There appear to be no corresponding organizational structures in the Soviet Union and China.) The corresponding American organization has the quaint name Association for Computing Machinery (ACM, for short). These names present a perplexing aspect only if taken literally in terms of current semantics. Currently the term *computer* is a synonym for "computing machine." But the British organization is not a group of computing machines. The name of the Canadian organization gives no clue that the computational aspect of information processing is its overwhelming concern. The name of the French organization reflects the French taste for the *pot pourri* or the universal aspect, depending upon your point of view; *cybernetics* is the science of automatic control, and *its* definition does not necessarily invoke the computer. The name of the American organization is not meant to suggest that there exists an Association against Computing Machinery (although there is—not so named—such a group and the authors of some of the references belong to it). And so on.

The academic segment and the literate part of the industrial segment of computerdom communicate among themselves through technical journals, and trade newspapers.

A fairly representative sample of the list of journals is the following:

Algorytmy
Australian Computer Journal
BIT
Communications of the ACM
Computer Journal
Computing
Computing Reviews
Computing Surveys
EIK
Elektronische Datenverarbeitung

IEEE Transactions on Electronic Computers
IEEE Transactions on System Science and Cybernetics
Information and Control
Information Processing
Information Sciences
International Journal of Computer Mathematics
International Journal of Man-Machine Studies
IBM System Journal
IBM Journal of Research and Development
Journal of Computer and System Sciences
Kybernetik
Linguistik und Informationsverarbeitung
Mathematics of Computation
Mathematical System Theory
Numerische Mathematik
Proceedings of the American Society for Information Sciences
Revue de Traitement de l'Information
Systems and Procedures Journal
USSR Computer Mathematics and Mathematical Physics

(This list might seem rather substantial, until it is realized that many articles dealing with the abstract aspect of computing appear sporadically in various mathematics journals—and there are about 1000 such journals.)

The trade journals tend to contain rather lightweight articles (usually devoted to commercial computer applications), richly interlarded with advertisements for the latest developments in the technology. The trade newspapers, of which perhaps the most notable is *Computerworld*, a weekly, carry newsy material related to computer applications, corporate developments, social implications of computer misuse, and of course carry their own heavy load of commercial advertisement. Their coverage of some of the fascinating mercantile machinations in the computer field tends to be broader than, but not as incisive as, say the *New York Times* or the *Wall Street Journal*.

The hard core of information about what is going on in computer science/ practice is to be found in the journals. If we look at the way ACM (in its *Computing Reviews*) catalogues the various facets of the subject, we find:

1. GENERAL TOPICS AND EDUCATION
   1.0 General
   1.1 Texts; Handbooks
   1.2 History; Biographies
   1.3 Introductory and Survey Articles
   1.4 Glossaries
   1.5 Education
   1.9 Miscellaneous
2. COMPUTING MILIEU
   2.0 General
   2.1 Philosophical and Social Implications
   2.2 Professional Aspects
   2.3 Legislation; Regulations
   2.4 Administration of Computing Centers
   2.9 Miscellaneous
3. APPLICATIONS
   3.0 General
   3.1 Natural Sciences
   3.2 Engineering
   3.3 Social and Behavioral Sciences
   3.4 Humanities
   3.5 Management Data Processing
   3.6 Artificial Intelligence
   3.7 Information Retrieval
   3.8 Real Time Systems
   3.9 Miscellaneous
4. PROGRAMMING
   4.0 General
   4.1 Processors
   4.2 Programming Languages
   4.3 Supervisory Systems
   4.4 Utility Programs
   4.5 Miscellaneous

5. MATHEMATICS OF COMPUTATION
    5.0 General
    5.1 Numerical Analysis
    5.2 Metatheory
    5.3 Combinatorial & Discrete Mathematics
    5.4 Mathematical Programming
    5.5 Mathematical Statistics; Probability
    5.6 Information Theory
    5.9 Miscellaneous

6. DESIGN AND CONSTRUCTION
    6.0 General
    6.1 Logical Design, Switching Theory
    6.2 Computer Systems
    6.3 Components and Circuits
    6.9 Miscellaneous

7. ANALOG COMPUTERS
    7.0 General
    7.1 Applications
    7.2 Design, Construction
    7.3 Hybrid Systems
    7.4 Programming, Techniques
    7.9 Miscellaneous

Of the seven major categories upon which ACM bases its abstracting strategy, we shall touch upon the first six. (The subject of analog computers, while interesting, is ancillary to the subject of digital computers.) Note that these categories tell us, not so much what computer science is, but rather what computer people do. The design and manufacture of computers is a delicate and complex matter that seems to fall squarely within the purview of electrical engineers. So clearly the art of building computers is *not* what computer science is all about—although almost every computer scientist is fascinated by the subject. The naive notion persistently presents itself: Perhaps computer science is the science of the application of computers, a combination of the theory of applied and abstract computation—in which case it might fall within the purview of mathematicians. After all, computers were invented to solve mathematical problems. The first abstract computer was invented to solve a problem in logic.

The question of the relationship of computer science to mathematics seems to be a curiously persistent preoccupation of the scientific establishment. George E. Forsythe (Chairman of the Computer Science Department at Stanford University) has said:

> ... I am told that the preponderant opinion among administrators in Washington is that computer science is part of applied mathematics. I believe the majority of university computer scientists would say it is not.*

One reason why computer scientists might say it is not, is that while mathematics is an encompassing and flexible science, many departments of mathematics are rigidly structured and tend to resist the considerable reorganization which is required to adjoin the equivalent of a department of computer science. This resistance tends to be bolstered by competition for the available budget and sometimes by certain attitudes of academic provincialism. (The latter tend to be both less humorous and more serious than Polya's little parable on observational ability.†) The result of these exclusionary influences has been the creation of computer science departments in many of the major universities. (But of course in the beginning these departments were mainly staffed by mathematicians.)

Once computer science departments come into existence, there arises the problem: What do they teach? Clearly mathematics can be

---

* G. E. Forsythe, "What to do till the computer scientist comes," *American Mathematical Monthly* **75** (1968), 454–462. This excerpt and the one following are reprinted by permission.

† In Volume I of *Induction and Analogy in Mathematics*, G. Polya has a logician observing a mathematician who, having noted that the first ninety-nine numbers are less than 100, infers by induction that all numbers are less than 100. The mathematician, in turn, proffers the case of a physicist who believes that 60 is divisable by all numbers: He finds it true of 1, 2, 3, 4, 5 and 6 and furthermore true of several more numbers—10, 20, and 30—taken at random, and so considers the experimental evidence complete. The physicist counters by citing an engineer who suspected all odd numbers to be prime: Upon checking the odd numbers up to 13, he found the supposition to be true—except for 9, which he ascribed to experimental error.

dispensed with. As for applied mathematics, Forsythe says:

> I must emphasize that the amount of computing done for applied mathematics is an almost invisible fraction of the total amount of computing today.
>
> . . . [the] Committee on the Support of Research in the Mathematical Sciences [COSRIMS] . . . has taken the position that computer science is a mathematical science, but many of the discussions emphasize differences between mathematics and computer science.

And as for pure mathematics, R. W. Hamming, of the Bell Telephone Laboratories, in his 1968 ACM Turing lecture, offered the following Agnew-like rhetoric on the subject:

> . . . We need to avoid the bragging of uselessness and game-playing that the pure mathematicians so often engage in. Whether or not the pure mathematician is right in claiming that what is utterly useless today will be useful tomorrow (and I doubt very much that he is, in the current situation), it is simply poor propaganda for raising the large amounts of money we need to support the continuing growth of the field. We need to avoid making computer science look like pure mathematics: Our primary standard for acceptance should be experience in the real world, not aesthetics.*

As for mathematics as a peripheral adjunct to the computer science curriculum, Hamming also has some advice:

> . . . I would also require a strong minor in some field *other* than mathematics . . . I believe we should avoid turning out more idiot savants—we have more than enough "computniks" now to last us a long time. What we need are professionals!

The university curriculum in computer science may be compelled to conform to what Robert M. Hutchins once called the "trade-school format."

---

* R. W. Hamming, "One man's view of computer science," *Journal ACM* **16** (1969), 3–12. Copyright © 1969, Association for Computing Machinery, Inc. This excerpt and the one following are reprinted by permission.

The graduates of that curriculum currently find themselves in an economic scene consisting of a large near-vertical rock; there is a view of unknown quality at the top, and an undesirable void at the bottom—and relatively few finger-holds in between. Supplying graduates with a workable set of academic pitons may be one of the economic necessities of life, if a life on the rock is their fate. And of course "computer science" will bend whatever the generic curriculum becomes. For the present, it seems that computer science is so formless that almost anything said about it is likely to be true. As a model for this axiom, we offer Allen Newell's memorandum to COSRIMS:

> Computer science shares with mathematics a concern with formalism and a concern with the manipulation of symbols. It also shares with mathematics the role of handmaiden to all of science and technology. It shares with electrical engineering the concern with the design and construction of information processing systems that accomplish ends.
>
> It shares with all of engineering a concern with the process of design, considered as an intellectual endeavor. It shares with linguistics a concern with language and communication. It shares with psychology a special concern with forms of information processing that result in intelligent behavior, broadly viewed. It shares with the library sciences a concern with how to store and retrieve large amounts of information, either as documents or as facts. It has both theoretical aspects, as in the study of automata, and experimental ones, as in the discovery of new types of systems through programming them and exploring their behavior. All of these shared problems with other parts of science and technology imply that the future status of computer science is still indeterminate. It may permanently become one of the mathematical sciences. It may become an autonomous science, such as geology. The result is genuinely in doubt, because "science" is a social construct, shaped as much by social forces as by anything intrinsic to its subject matter.*

---

* Reprinted by permission from *The Mathematical Sciences: A Report*, Publication 1681, Committee on Support of Research in the Mathematical Sciences—National Research Council, National Academy of Sciences, Washington, D.C., 1968.

REFERENCES

Forsythe, G. E. (1968), What to do till the computer scientist comes, *American Mathematical Monthly* **75**, 454–462.

Freeman, R. B. (1971), *The Market for College-Trained Manpower. A Study in the Economics of Career Choice*. Cambridge: Harvard University Press.

Jackson, J. A. (1970), *Professions and Professionalisation*. New York: Cambridge University Press.

Luehrmann, A. W. (1971), *Proceedings of the Second Annual Conference on Computers in the Undergraduate Curricula*. Hanover, N.H.: The University Press of New England.

McKenney, J. L. and F. M. Tonge (1971), The state of computer oriented curricula in business schools 1970, *Communications of the ACM* **14**, 443–448.

Minsky, M. (1970), Form and content in computer science, *Journal of the ACM* **17**, 197–215.

Teichroew, D. ed. (1971), Education related to the use of computers in organizations, *Communications of the ACM* **14**, 573–588; this paper contains an unusually extended and useful bibliography.

Wegner, P. (1970), Three computer cultures: computer technology, computer mathematics, and computer science, *Advances in Computers* **10**, 7–78.

Wolfle D. and C. V. Kidd (1971), The future market for Ph.D.'s, *Science* **173**, 784–793.

2 Computer Pre-history: 1663 and all that

My wife rose anon, and she and I all afternoon at arithmetique, and she able to additions, subtractions and multiplications very well, and so I purpose not to trouble her yet with divisions. . .

Pepys, 1663

It is unworthy of excellent men to lose hours like slaves in the labor of calculations which could safely be relegated to anyone else if machines were used. . .

Leibniz, 1671

. . . .

The precursor of the digital computer is the abacus—the word perhaps derives from the semitic word *abq* for dust—the first step in the mechanization of computation which was a simple realization of the computational processes pursued on dust trays or sand trays. The rod numerals* used by the Chinese for supposedly the millenium B.C. and represented in calculation by ivory or bamboo rods almost suggest the

---

* In this set of numerals,

$$|, \, ||, \, |||, \, ||||, \, ||||, \, \text{T}, \, \text{T}, \, \text{T}, \, \text{TT}$$

represent the numbers 1 to 9, and the numerals

$$-, =, \equiv, \overline{\equiv}, \overline{\overline{\equiv}}, \perp, \perp, \perp, \perp$$

represent the first nine multiples of 10. These two types can be alternated to give numbers of arbitrary size (e.g., $-|-|$ represents 1, 111).

form of the abacus, a rigid frame in which are set parallel wires on which ride beads used as markers.

As a ubiquitous computing device, the abacus has stood the test of time. Its principal competitor has been—from the time of its invention in 1622 by the English mathematician William Oughtred—the slide rule. (But the slide rule is an analogue, rather than a digital, computing device and hereafter we snub such mechanisms.) The counting board, or abacus, was known perhaps as early to the Arabs, and the Romans and Greeks, as it was to the Chinese. In any case it was an important device and remained so, for example in Europe, until about the sixteenth century when its need faded when a general facility for working with the Hindu-Arabic numerals came into play.

A notable boost to computing ability occurred in 1614 when the Scottish part-time mathematician John Napier published his invention of the logarithm, after having worked on the notion for twenty years. The next year, John Briggs, a professor of geometry at Oxford, visited Napier, and they agreed on the form that a table of logarithms should take. In 1617 Briggs published a table of logarithms (to base 10) of the numbers 1 to 1000, computed to fourteen places. (A table of natural logarithms calculated by John Speidell, was published in 1619.)

The French mathematician, Blaise Pascal, built the first mechanical computer in 1642. Pascal was a mathematical prodigy, published a short (but important) paper at the age of sixteen, became a calculator designer at eighteen, and a computer entrepreneur at twenty. He built and sold about fifty of his adding machines within a period of several years, and then went back to the more respectable pursuit of mathematics.

Gottfried Wilhelm von Leibniz entered the University of Leipzig at the age of fifteen, studied mathematics, philosophy, law and theology, and received his bachelor's degree after two years of study. At the age of twenty he was prepared for the degree of doctor of laws, but the generation gap was rather severe at that time (1666) and the degree was withheld because of his youth. He seems to have transferred his credits to the University of Altdorf at Nuremberg where he got the degree anyway and was even offered a professorship. He refused this and elected to do a tour in the diplomatic service. Political missions took him to London in 1673 and again in 1676 (thus bracketing the years in Paris when he invented *his* version of the calculus), and on this second visit Leibniz brought along a calculating machine which he had built in 1673. Leibniz's calculator was an improvement over that of Pascal in that the Leibniz machine was a stepped wheel which could perform multiplication by rapid iteration of addition. Despite Leibniz's doctrine that this is the best of all possible worlds—a view that provoked Voltaire's *Candide*—his machine failed to function reliably in it. Still, Leibniz's successes in mathematics and physics were so profound, that the malfunctions of his cameo computer are a matter of indifference. (In any case, the fault lay not in the design but in the construction—as was to be the case in so many computers yet to come.)

It is hard to guess how many designs for such miniature mechanical calculators were realized during the seventeenth and eighteenth centuries. That history records so few is due probably to the fact that many of the designers failed to enjoy the reputation of a Pascal or a Leibniz, coupled with the fact that the machines failed to work adequately. But every once in a while news of the discovery of yet another model is heard—like the surfacing of a kind of computational Dead Sea scroll. For example, *Mathematical Reviews* [September 1970] contains a review by C. J. Scriba of an article written by L. E. Maistrov and V. L. Cenekal appearing in a Russian journal* devoted to the history of science:

A very old calculating machine (Russian)

The authors report on a calculating machine for four species, built by an otherwise unknown Hebrew clockmaker and mechanic Jewna Jacobson at Nieswiez, province of Minsk, Lithuania, probably not later than 1770. The mechanism of the machine is contained in a rectangular box measuring 34.2 by 21.8 by 3.4 cm. The scales and driving axes are assembled on the top side of the box, which also is attractively decorated and carries some inscriptions: "Mechanische Rechnungs Maschine; Maschina Mechaniszna do Rachunku [German and Polish]. Zu der Aufgabe des Addirens, Subtantirens, Multiplicirens, und Dividirens von den Nummer

---

* *Voprosy Istor. Estestvoznan. i Tehn. Vyp.* 1 (26) (1969), 35–39.

Eins bis zu Tausend Millionen und übrig bleibt von der Division und das kann man hier in den Bruchen zertheilen. Erfunden und verfertiget von dem Hebreer Jewna Jacobson, Uhrmacher und Mechanicus in der Stadt Nieswiez in Lithauen, Gouvernement Minsk." Operations with this calculating machine are limited to numbers with at most nine digits. It is obvious, however, from the signs of usage, that the machine was mostly—and for a long time—employed for the computation of numbers with no more than five digits.

Apart from scales whose sole purpose is to store a given number or an intermediate result, the core of the mechanism contained in the box consists of a row of nine cogged wheels, one for each digit. Each of these can be turned into ten positions (representing the figures 0, 1, 2, . . ., 9, which can be seen through windows in the cover) by means of a pair of semicircular discs equipped with nine special teeth. One of these semi-circular discs, placed on one side of the cog-wheel, will turn it clockwise (addition); the other, placed on the other side, will turn it counterclock-wise (subtraction). The said discs (18 in all) were driven in clockwise direction from the outside by help of a key or little crank that is now lost. When released, the discs would return into their original position (with-out moving the main cog-wheels, of course) thanks to built-in springs. For transmission from units to tens, from tens to hundreds, etc., on each cog-wheel is mounted an extra long cog which (by the help of another cog-wheel necessary to convey clockwise rotation into clockwise rota-tion) will pass the motion from one place to the next higher whenever the sum in a single digit is greater than nine.

Division is effected as repeated subtraction, the number of subtractions carried out being counted by nine additional discs—one for each digit again. Each of these circular discs carries ten spikes corresponding to the ten digits visible through a window. Whenever the semi-disc for sub-traction belonging to it is put into motion, it will turn this disc by one spike, i.e., by 36°. In fact, it seems to be for this reason that the "wheels" driving the main cog-wheels are given the shape of semi-discs. According to the authors, this counting mechanism and the semi-discs are Jacobson's original invention.*

---

* From *Mathematical Reviews*, Review#2503, Volume 40, No. 3, Sept. 1970. Reprinted by permission.

The miniature engines of Pascal, Leibniz, and the Lithuanian clock maker were fascinating but rudimentary devices. It was at the next, critical, stage of developments that the universal computer—at least in chrysalis form—emerged. The inventor of this remarkable instrument—as well as the architect and engineer of its near-realization—was the Englishman Charles Babbage. As Dr. Dionysius Lardner put it, writing in the *Edinburgh Review* of July, 1834:

> ... Mr. Babbage selected science as the field of his ambition; and his mathematical researches have conferred on him a high reputation, wherever the exact sciences are studied and appreciated. The suffrages of the mathematical world have been ratified in his own country, where he has been elected to the Lucasian Professorship in his own University—a chair, which, though of inconsiderable emolument, is one on which Newton has conferred everlasting celebrity.
>
> But it has been the fortune of this mathematician to surround himself with fame of another and more popular kind, and which rarely falls to the lot of those who devote their lives to the cultivation of the abstract sciences. This distinction he owes to the announcement, some years since, of his celebrated project of a Calculating Engine. A proposition to reduce arithmetic to the dominion of mechanism—to substitute an automation for a compositor—to throw the powers of thought into wheelwork could not fail to awaken the attention of the world.

Babbage was an eccentric, in the best sense of the word. B. V. Bowden, in his *Brief History of Computation**, says that Babbage had taught himself mathematics so well that when he went to Cambridge University (at the age of eighteen), "he found to his dismay that he knew more algebra than his tutor." Discontent with the state of mathematical affairs at Cambridge, Babbage together with two other young activists (the mathematician George Peacock and the astronomer John Herschel), formed an organization called the Analytical Society, a device through which they intended to restructure the teaching of mathematics and

---

* *Faster Than Thought: A symposium on Digital Computing Machines*, ed. B. V. Bowden. Sir Isaac Pitman & Sons, London, 1953.

bring the English presentation of the calculus onto par with the Leibnizian developments on the continent.

Babbage arrived at Cambridge in 1810. (He was elected to the Lucasian Chair of Mathematics in 1828, and, according to Bowden, "he established another precedent by holding the office for eleven years without ever giving a lecture in the University.") Babbage says that (in 1812)*:

> ... One evening I was sitting in the rooms of the Analytical Society, at Cambridge, my head leaning forward on the table in a kind of dreamy mood, with a table of logarithms lying open before me. Another member, coming into the room, and seeing me half asleep, called out, "Well, Babbage, what are you dreaming about?" to which I replied, "I am thinking that all these Tables (pointing to the logarithms) might be calculated by machinery."

The computation of tables (of logarithms, sines, cosines) was the primary impetus for Babbage's conception of a calculating engine. Such tables were crucial to much of the primitive technology of the times. (One student of history has claimed, perhaps cynically, that the table of logarithms and the all-tile bathroom were the basis of modern civilization.) Such tables as existed then (early nineteenth century) were riddled with errors; one of the notable characteristics of human behavior is an apparently unsuppressible tendency to deviate from the rules—even when there is conscientious intent not to do so. And those whose humdrum task it was to grind out calculations of tables of functions were no exception.

Babbage's idea of his Difference Engine was an entirely natural one: Since there is a fixed, mechanical procedure whereby one calculates such tables of functions, why not in fact have a *machine* perform the procedure? (Such calculations are usually performed using techniques from the theory of finite differences—hence the name Difference Engine.)

---

* *Charles Babbage and his Calculating Engines: Selected Writings by Charles Babbage and Others*, ed. Philip Morrison and Emily Morrison. Dover, Publications Inc. New York, 1961.

Starting with this notion, it seems to have taken Babbage about twenty years to realize that, with relatively slight generalizations in the design of the Difference Engine, he could obtain a more powerful calculating device: a machine which was capable of performing not just finite difference calculations but indeed seemingly all of the algorithms of mathematics ("analysis"). (About 100 years later, a Harvard physicist, Howard Aiken, went through this same cycle of generalization in his design of a mechanical-relay version of what Babbage was attempting to create with geared wheels.) To the machine which would perform all the algorithms of analysis, Babbage gave the name Analytical Engine.

A key idea in Babbage's conception of how a calculating engine should work held that the machine should be supplied with a program that would control its sequence of operations without human intervention during the course of calculation. As a device for presenting the program to the machine, Babbage chose the medium of punched cards already used in 1801 by Joseph Jacquard for the automatic control of looms in weaving.

Although Babbage was a prolific writer, the best account of his designs for the Engines was provided by an Italian military engineer, L. F. Menebrea, who attended some lectures given by Babbage at the military college in Turin in 1840. Menebrea, fascinated by the concept of the Analytical Engine, published his version of the material in French two years later (in the *Bibliothèque Universelle de Genève*, 1842). This, in turn, was translated into English by Ada Augusta Byron (daughter of Lord Byron and later the Countess of Lovelace). Lady Lovelace's translation, together with some extended and impressive notes of her own, appears as an appendix in Bowden's book. Lady Lovelace, twenty five years Babbage's junior, grasped at once, upon introduction to the machines, the principles of their design and provided a clear and competent account of them. She had had some fairly good mathematical training—her tutor was the logician De Morgan—and a mind keen enough to take advantage of it. According to Bowden, De Morgan's estimate of her ability was high:

> . . . he said of her that had she been a man, her "aptitude for grasping the strong points and the real difficulties of first principles would

have lowered her chance of being senior wrangler, but would have made her into an original mathematical investigator, perhaps of first rate eminence."

Her notes on Menebrea's article contain some sophisticated results and what may have been the first programs written for a computer. She not only gave clearcut presentations of what the Engines were all about, but also undertook to help Babbage in his continuing and occasionally desperate search for financial support for the construction of the Engines*.

The hazard of relying upon government support in scientific endeavors is well known, and Babbage's case was a classic. Initially his support came about because the Royal Society was impressed with a small demonstration model of the Difference Engine. At the recommendation of the Royal Society, the Chancellor of the Exchequer promised to subsidize a more powerful model. But in the course of development of a full-scale version, Babbage several times changed the design and intended capacity of the machine, intending finally to realize the Analytical Engine rather than the Difference Engine. At this crucial stage, the government withdrew support, and thereafter efforts of the Royal Society urging the government to change its course were of no avail. Babbage's personal fortune, which he had expended on development of the machines, dwindled, and neither Difference Engine nor Analytical Engine was completed in what Babbage visualized as its final form.

The critical evaluation of Cambridge, which motivated Babbage during his student years to help found the Analytical Society, was repeated in later years but now focused on the Royal Society and the government. The government, he felt, had failed badly in supporting science, and the agency most responsible in this failure was the Royal Society. As for the Society itself, he had formulated some reforms "to rescue it from con-

---

* Babbage and Lady Lovelace apparently collaborated on a strategy for winning at the track. The mathematics may have been right, but the horses were wrong. Babbage, after a while, decided he could not take the losses and pulled out, but Lady Lovelace persisted, and lost her shirt.

tempt in our own country, and ridicule in others." Among other reforms, he recommended a record of publication of scientific articles as a qualification for membership in the Society, democratic election of officers, and open discussion of Society policies. The Society rejected his proposal without discussion.

Babbage also held the Royal Society responsible for what he considered abominable administration of the Royal Observatory at Greenwich. Astronomical tables were a prime candidate for automation and Babbage at one point tried to obtain a copy of the Greenwich observations and was refused. Pursuing the matter, he found that Airy, the Astronomer Royal, had sold five tons of the *Greenwich Tables* to be resold for pasteboard. According to Bowden:

> Babbage remarked acidly that no one was better fitted than the Astronomer Royal to decide what should be done with his observations, but he doubted if it were possible to devise a more extravagant method of remunerating a public official than to set up an observatory and a computing center and to produce and print astronomical tables merely as a source of wastepaper.

Airy, by virtue of his position, was Scientific Advisor to the Queen and in that capacity recommended both against mechanizing the computation of the *Greenwich Tables* and against further subsidy of the Difference Engine.

Talent and energy, in this case, were no compensation for financial deprivation. Had the support been continued, Babbage's grand design might have been realized as a completed working model of the Analytical Engine. But the failure to complete this development still leaves with undiminished luster Babbage's vision of what *could* be built as a universal machine. As for the general uncertainty that met this vision, Lady Lovelace said:

> The Difference Engine, however, appears to us to be in a great measure an answer to these doubts. It is complete as far as it goes, and it does work with all the anticipated success. The Analytical Engine, far from being more complicated, will in many respects be of simpler construction; and it is a remarkable circumstance attending it, that with very *simplified* means it is so much more powerful.

Just how simple and how powerful a calculating engine could be was settled about one hundred years later by the English logician Turing, as we shall next see.

REFERENCES

Babbage, C. (1864), *Passages from the Life of a Philosopher*. London: Longman, Green, Longman, Roberts & Green.

Bowden, B. V. (1953), *Faster Than Thought, A Symposium on Digital Computing Machines*. London: Pitman.

von Mackensen, L. (1969), *Zur Vorgeschichte und Entstehung der ersten digitalen 4-Spezies-Rechenmaschine von Gottfried Wilhelm Leibniz*, Studia Leibnitiana Supplementa, Vol. II. Wiesbaden: Franz Steiner Verlag GMBH.

Morrison, P. and E. (1961), *Charles Babbage and his Calculating Engines*. New York: Dover.

Roth, L. (1971), Old Cambridge days, *American Mathematical Monthly* **78**, 223–236.

3 Turing's Mini Super-computer

. . . The first professor I saw was in a very large Room, with Forty Pupils about him. After Salutation, observing me to look earnestly upon a Frame, which took up the greatest part of both the Length and Breadth of the Room; he said, perhaps I might wonder to see him employed in a Project for improving speculative Knowledge by practical and mechanical Operations . . .

Everyone knew how laborious the usual Method is of attaining to Arts and Sciences; whereas by his Contrivance, the most ignorant Person at a reasonable Charge, and with a little bodily Labour, may write Books in Philosophy, Poetry, Politicks, Law, Mathematicks, and Theology, without the least Assistance from Genius or Study. He then led me to the Frame, about the sides whereof all his Pupils stood in Ranks. It was Twenty Foot square . . . linked together by slender Wires. These Bits . . . were covered on every Square with Paper pasted upon them; and on these Papers were written all the Words of their Language . . .

The Professor then desired me to observe, for he was going to set his Engine at work. The Pupils at his Command took each of them hold of an Iron Handle, whereof there were Forty fixed round the Edges of the Frame; and giving them a sudden Turn, the whole Disposition of the Words was entirely changed . . .

I made my humblest Acknowledgements to this illustrious Person . . . and promised if ever I had the good Fortune to return to my native Country, that I would do him Justice, as the sole Inventor of this wonderful Machine . . .

Jonathan Swift, *Gulliver's Travels*

. . . .

Babbage's conception of the Difference Engine was that of a powerful, practical-in-principle machine which was conceived too soon—in an era when its realization was impractical. About 100 years later—in the 1930s—the English mathematician Alan Turing formulated a concept of an abstract computer which is marvelously simple, yet qualitatively more powerful than any real computer could be. Such a device is known as a Turing machine. Before considering a particular example, we should note the way in which the structures of real computers and the structures of Turing machines differ.

A real digital computer has a memory of, say, perhaps 30,000 cells, and each of these cells can hold a number of, say, at most 15 digits in length. Among the instructions which the computer can accept are those of the form:

a) Place the number k in cell C_i.

b) Make a copy of the number in cell C_i and place the copy in cell C_j.

c) Add the number in cell C_i to the number in cell C_j and place the result in cell C_k.

d) Multiply the number in cell C_i by the number in cell C_j and place the result in cell C_k.

e) If the number in cell C_i is zero, then do ... (some instruction); if the number in cell C_i is not zero, then do ... (some other instruction).

The limitation on the power of actual computers stems from the fact that, in instructions of the form (a), a number which is to be placed in a cell can be at most (in this example) 15 digits long. Now a maximum of 15 digits in length may seem quite generous—until we want to multiply two 15-digit numbers and then we wish we had a computer which had cells that could hold 30-digit numbers.

Another kind of difficulty occurs in the use of instructions of the form (c) and (d). We might wish to compute some sequence of numbers, placing the first number x_1 in cell C_1, the second number x_2 in cell C_2, and so on ..., with the intention of performing some operation on this sequence, once we have it. But the difficulty comes when 30,000 numbers have been generated and all the cells are in use.

There are some obvious ways out of these difficulties. For example, when there are numbers too large to store in a cell, why not store the spill-over in another cell? (Of course this cuts down the number of available cells.) And if the number of available cells is too small, build (or buy) a memory of twice the size. But, clearly, sooner or later some physical (or financial) limit is going to be reached and we are stuck with a computer which is perhaps very large—but nevertheless finite!

The Turing machine has an infinite memory and all the power that goes with it. Instead of a finite array of cells, it has an infinite array; and, to keep things simple, each Turing machine cell holds just one digit (or is blank). Turing visualized this array of cells as an infinite tape, marked off into squares, each such square being capable of holding just one digit (or other useful symbol) or else being blank. The collection of symbols which a particular Turing machine uses is called the *alphabet* of the machine and is a fixed, finite set of symbols.

If we assume that the Turing machine tape holds (just) the number 1011, we might regard the tape as looking like: ... ***********1011 ***********
..., where * denotes the blank and the string of periods ("....") is used to indicate that the leftmost string of blanks extends infinitely far to the left and the rightmost string of blanks extends infinitely far to the right.

The "hardware" of the Turing machine consists of a read-write head and a built-in program. The read-write head can scan one cell (i.e., square) at a time; then, depending upon the "state" of the machine and the symbol which the machine happens to be scanning, the read-write head will move either to the cell to the left, or to the cell to the right, or will first replace the symbol being scanned by a new symbol and then move to the left or to the right. As it moves to the adjacent cell, it will change to another—perhaps the same—state and then go through the cycle again— unless it has changed to the *stop* state. Consider the machine which adds unity to whatever number it finds on its tape, and then stops. Its program might look like:

In state	Scanning symbol	Print symbol	Move	Adopt state
1	0	0	right	1
1	1	1	right	1
1	*	*	left	2
2	0	1	left	3
2	1	0	left	2
2	*	1	left	stop
3	0	0	left	3
3	1	1	left	3
3	*	*	left	stop

The instructions which this program represents are carried out by the machine in the following way:

If the machine, scanning a certain symbol while in a certain state, finds this state-symbol combination in the box at the left, the machine proceeds in accordance with the corresponding line in the box at the right. For example, the first line of the program says (in effect): When in state 1, scanning symbol 0, the action to be effected is replace the symbol, under scan, by 0 and move right, changing to state 1 in the process. (Of course, the next effect of this instruction is simply to move the read-write head to the adjacent symbol on the right, without changing anything else.)

The usual convention for starting the computation of a Turing machine is to set it in state 1 with its read-write head scanning the first non-blank symbol on the tape, and then to press the *go* button. We can follow the action of this particular machine on the tape ... ***1011 ***... by showing the tape after each move of the machine and by writing, above the symbol under scan, the state in which the machine finds itself at that point. If we do this, then we get the following picture of how the computation goes:

A Computation by a Machine Which Adds One

```
        1
... ***1011 ***...
        1
... ***1011 ***...
```

```
        1
... ***1011 ***...
        1
... ***1011 ***...
         1
... ***1011 ***...
         2
... ***1011 ***...
         2
... ***1010 ***...
         2
... ***1000 ***...
        3
... ***1100 ***...

... ***1100 ***...
```

Notice that the action of the machine is to move the read-write head to the right, searching for the first blank square and maintaining the same state and leaving the just-scanned symbol intact; when the end of the number 1011 is discovered, the machine sends the read-write head to the left, changing each symbol along the way in accordance with the rules for adding unity to a number (in binary notation). A curious bit of behavior shown by this machine is its action when started on a completely blank tape. (Adding unity to nothing at all is not the same as adding unity to zero, so we are confronting the machine with a nonsensical situation— and so perhaps we should not be particularly surprised by *anything* which it then does.) According to the program, the machine, starting on a blank square, moves left, writes 1, and stops! (It is easy to write a program, only slightly more complicated than the one given here, which, starting the machine on a blank symbol, immediately stops without having changed the tape at all—perhaps an aesthetically more appealing machine.)

The machine is this example shares a finiteness property of all Turing machines: Its number of states must be finite and its alphabet must be finite; only its storage capacity (i.e., its tape) may be infinite. Can a Turing machine with a big alphabet or a big set of states do something that a Turing machine with a small alphabet or a small set of states cannot do? Roughly speaking, the answer is "no." If a machine M has an alphabet consisting of symbols $s_1, s_2, \ldots, s_n$, then we can recode these symbols, using only the alphabet consisting of 0 and 1, by using 101 for the code of s_1, using 1001 for the code of s_2, 10001 for the code of s_3, and so on. Note that if M's tape were, for example,

$$\ldots *** s_3\ s_1\ s_2\ s_2\ s_1\ *** \ldots$$

then a tape which is the coded version of the above tape, would look like:

$$\ldots *** 10001101100110011001 *** \ldots$$

It turns out that we can design a Turing machine M' which will do a computation, equivalent to that of M, but with a $(0,1)$-coded tape. So a very big alphabet does not permit, in principle, the computation of anything that cannot be computed by a corresponding machine with a rather small alphabet (although the *efficiency* of computation by the machine with the larger alphabet might be better).

As for a machine with a very large number of states, it turns out that again it is possible to design a machine that performs equivalent computations but which has only *two* states (and a much larger alphabet).

One of Turing's contributions was to show that there is a particular machine—it is suggestive to call it a "universal" Turing machine*— which, when presented with a tape on which is a pair of numbers, say p and q, will perform a computation the result of which is just what a Turing machine P would compute when P's tape contains the number q—provided that p is the code of the machine P. How can we code a machine? First we need a pair of reserved symbols, for punctuation, and we shall use the bracket symbols] and [for these. Next we write the program of any particular Turing machine as a single string of symbols.

---

* The smallest universal Turing machine (if "size" is measured by the product of the number of states and the number of symbols) that anyone, so far, has formulated is due to Minsky: It has seven states and four symbols. In contrast a typical computer has of the order of a million states and about as many symbols as a typewriter keyboard.

For example, we can write the add-one-in-binary program as

100R1] 111R1] 1**L2] 201L3] 210L2]2*1LS]300L3]311L3]3**LS][

where we replace the words *right*, *left*, and *stop* by symbols R, L, and S, respectively we then write the first line of the (resulting) program, followed by the symbol] and then the second line of the program, followed by the symbol], and so on, until the entire program has been written down. Finally we write the symbol [(as the equivalent of a period). We require eight symbols for this encoding (that is, 0, 1, L, R, S, *,], and [ ). We regard these as the alphabet s_1, s_2,..,s_8 and replace each such symbol s_i by its $(0,1)$-code 1000..01 (with i occurrences of 0, flanked at beginning and end by 1). The resulting number, a string of 0's and 1's, we regard as the code p of the machine P.

A notable aspect of this procedure is that it can be used to code not just machines but any sentence in any finite alphabet. (Of course the alphabet must be fixed in advance.) And, from the number which is the code of the sentence, we can always recover the original sentence itself. (This trick of converting nonnumerical strings to numbers and back again—not necessarily in the particular way used above—is due to a famous logician, Kurt Gödel*, and the numbers obtained as codes are called, appropriately, Gödel numbers.)

A corollary of this ability to cast nonnumerical strings into a numerical form is that various procedures can be applied to such strings by writing programs that perform the corresponding numerical operations on the corresponding numerical codes. This is just another way of saying something that is already well known. The computer is capable of considerably more data processing than just the computation of values of functions. (Of course, so far as the computer is concerned it *is* just computing the

---

* Gödel showed that for any well-defined system of mathematical axioms there exist mathematical questions that cannot be settled on the basis of these axioms. Harvard, honoring him in 1952 for this demonstration that mathematics is "inexhaustible," phrased the citation: "Discoverer of the most significant mathematical truth of this century, incomprehensible to laymen, revolutionary for philosophers and logicians."

values of functions; that is, it may not "know" the identity of the objects whose codes are the numbers which the computer is processing.)

Turing made another remarkable contribution by showing that a rather simple-sounding problem about Turing machines is unsolvable (by any other Turing machine).* The problem is the *halting problem* for Turing machines: Is there some Turing machine T which, when presented with the code of any Turing machine M, can (from its computation) decide whether M would, if started computing on an empty tape, ultimately stop computing? First of all, what do we mean here by "decide"? Just that the Turing machine T would stop computing with its tape of the form ... ********0***** ... if the answer is "*yes*," or of the form ... ********1******** ... if the answer is "*no*." It might be thought (since the add-one-in-binary machine, above, when started on an empty tape, computes and then stops) that perhaps every Turing machine would finally stop if started on an empty tape; but this is not so, since the machine M' with the program

State	Symbol		Symbol	Move	State
I	0		0	right	stop
I	1		1	right	stop
I	*		*	right	I

when started on an empty tape, will search to the right forever, since it stops only upon encountering the symbol 0 or the symbol 1.

So the rules of the game that represent the will-it-ever-stop question are these: Given any Turing machine M we form the $(0,1)$-string $\overline{M}$ (as we shall call the code of M) and present the Turing machine T with the tape ... *******$\overline{M}$******** ... and T is to compute for a while and then stop; when T stops, T's tape is to look like either ... ******0******** ... or ... *******1******* ... (whichever is appropriate, corresponding to whether or not the machine M, when started on an empty tape, computes and finally stops or, alternately, computes forever). Turing showed that *no such machine T is possible.*

---

* Note the parallel to Gödel's result.

One might, at first glance, think that this is a result which simply emphasizes that Turing machines happen to have a curious inability to solve certain simple-sounding problems. But what lends a rather compelling importance to Turing's result is the belief—almost universal in the mathematical community—that if a Turing machine cannot solve a computational problem, then *no* calculational scheme *whatever* can solve the problem.* In other words, it's quite possible to be asked to construct a computer program that will solve a certain problem for which no such program can exist. The programmer then is in a predicament somewhat like that of the Sorcerer's Apprentice when his mentor was unavailable. And, as we all know, a good sorcerer is hard to find.

REFERENCES

Delong, H. (1971), Unsolved problems in arithmetic, *Scientific American* **224**, 50–60.

Gödel, K. (1931), Über formal unentscheidbare Satze der Principia Mathematica und verwandter Systeme, *Monatschefte der Mathematik und Physik* **38**, 173–198. (An English translation exists as *Kurt Gödel, On Formally Undecidable Propositions*, translation by B. Meltzer. New York;

---

* The German mathematician David Hilbert, early in this century, stated as a central problem of mathematical logic the task of finding a proof that an algorithm exists which can decide whether or not an arbitrary sentence of the predicate calculus is valid. In 1936 the logician Alonzo Church proposed a precise model of the notion of algorithm and showed that, if this model is used, there is no possible algorithm which can perform the required decision (i.e., solve the *Entscheidungsproblem*). Turing also gave an outline of a solution to the problem, using *his* model of algorithm, and it was shortly discovered that both models compute precisely the same class of functions (a class known as the class of partial recursive functions). Shortly after World War II, the Russian logician A. A. Markov proposed still another model (the normal algorithm), which was quickly seen to be equivalent to that of Turing. Programming languages, such as FORTRAN and ALGOL, are again models of the general notion of algorithm. And each of these models computes (in principle) exactly the same class of functions.

Basic Books, 1962.) A rather informal exposition of Gödel's result may also be found in "Gödel's Proof," by Ernest Nagel and J. R. Newman, in *The World of Mathematics* **3**, 1668−1695, New York: Simon & Shuster, 1956.

Markov, A. A. (1954), Theory of algorithms, *Proceedings of the Steklov Mathematical Institute*, vol. 42, Moscow (translation from the Russian for the Office of Technical Services, U.S. Dept of Commerce, Washington, D.C., 1961).

Minsky, M. (1967), *Computation: Finite and Infinite Machines*. New York: Prentice-Hall.

Traktenbrot, B. A. (1963), *Algorithms and Automatic Computing Machines* (translation from the Russian edition by J. Kristian, J. D. McCawley and S. A. Schmitt) Boston: D. C. Heath.

Turing, A. On computable numbers, with an application to the Entscheidungsproblem, *Proceedings of the London Mathematical Society*, *Series 2*, **42** (1936−1937), 230−265; corrections **43** (1937), 544−546. (The papers by Turing, along with a number of other important source papers by different authors, have been collected together in *The Undecidable*, ed. Martin Davis. Hewlett, New York: Raven Press 1965.) An account of Turing's life, told within the constraints of maternal discretion, is Sara Turing's *Alan M. Turing*, Cambridge: Heffer & Sons, 1959. A brief but engaging account of life with Turing as mathematician/administrator is given by J. H. Wilkinson in his 1970 ACM Turing Lecture, "Some comments from a numerical analyst," *Journal of the ACM* **18** (1971), 137−147.

4 The Road to Bitsville

Memorex has defined its corporate interests to encompass media and equipment products for information handling systems.

The development of our business thus reflects our pursuit of opportunities in information and data acquisition, preparation, communication, conversion, reduction, storage, retrieval, reproduction and display. These opportunities are manifold in the information explosion which is occurring throughout the world, and especially in data processing.*

Memorex Corporation
1969 Annual Report

. . . .

To read the golden, glistening prose which the computer industry splashes over its stock holders is to wonder whether the course of industrial research and development has the same smooth and glossy character. If one looks at the sequence of events that comprise the course of the American facet of the industrial computer development, one gets a sense of companies headed by men with a keen technological bent or men with a powerful grasp of the tactics and principles of sales aggression—but rarely a combination of the two. And many companies seem to have had neither. One gets an even stronger sense of the fact that, in the American scheme of things, success or failure is strictly determined by

---

* Reprinted by permission.

financial power. The example of Babbage, left hanging in a monetary limbo when the British government withdrew support, is repeated in comical correspondence in the case of several companies which appear in the following resume. We refer below, with the designation "[Rosen]", to the excellent survey article by Saul Rosen ("Electronic computers: a historical survey," *Computing Surveys* 1 (1969), 7–36), which contains an extensive bibliography; and we use the designation "[Rodgers]" to refer to the critical history of IBM written by William Rodgers (*THINK, A Biography of the Watsons and IBM*, Stein and Day, New York 1969). The designation "[Bowden]" is for the book by Bowden to which we have already referred.

In the following outline we give first the year in which work on a particular computer began, then the year in which it was completed, the designation of the machine, and its designer and constructors. The outline is not meant to be complete, but rather an indication of the pace of developments—largely on the American scene which, with some few but notable exceptions, was where the sprint took place.

1939/1943

Mark I (Automatic Sequence Controlled Calculator). Howard Aiken, while pursuing doctoral research at Harvard University, undertook to mechanize the work of calculating numerical approximations to differential equations. After inventing several variations on a machine to evaluate polynomials, he realized that these variations were, in their logical organization, much the same, and that a single general-purpose machine could be designed which would do the work of the various specialized machines. Thus Aiken went through the same cycle of generalization that Babbage had gone through a hundred years earlier. (The operating manual for the Mark I begins with the quotation from Babbage: "If, unwarned by my example, any man shall succeed in constructing an engine embodying in itself the whole of the executive department of mathematical analysis . . . I have no fear of leaving my reputation in his charge, for he alone will be able fully to appreciate the nature of my efforts and the value of their results.")

Discussions between Aiken and IBM led to IBM's construction of the Mark I at a cost of a million dollars. What resulted was a dinosaur of a machine, fifty one feet long and eight feet high, constructed of electromechanical (rather than electronic) components, and hence a machine already obsolete upon completion. It was, however, the first working realization of Babbage's concept of a universal computer.

1943/1946

ENIAC (Electronic Numerical Integrator and Calculator).   J. P. Eckert and John Mauchly designed and built this first electronic computer at the Moore School at the University of Pennsylvania. Although another dinosaur (weighing thirty tons), its nineteen thousand vacuum tubes gave it a speed many hundreds of times faster than the Mark I with its mechanical relays—and presumably it would have been considerably faster had its design relied upon binary, rather than decimal, circuitry. (Bowden, reviewing the machine in 1953, said: "It is ... probably the largest machine that will ever be built.") A capability which the machine lacked—and one which is critical for efficient use of a fast machine— was the facility for storing the program, embodying the calculation, in the memory of the machine. (Turing in 1936 had shown how the program could be encoded into the memory of his abstract universal computer, and the principle is just the same for electronic computers.)

In 1945 the eminent mathematician John von Neumann issued the draft of a report proposing the construction of a new computer, the EDVAC (Electronic Discrete Variable Computer), the design of which defined an operational model of the stored program computer. This type of computer required much more memory than was practical, using vacuum tubes as storage elements. Several different approaches were now undertaken to endow the machines with the additional necessary memory.

1947/1949

EDSAC (Electronic Delay Storage Automatic Computer). Professor Maurice Wilkes directed the construction of this machine at Cambridge University. Additional memory took the form of a mercury column acoustic delay line. This seems to be the first machine that actually operated as a stored program computer. The final stage of universalization of computers was complete.

1946/1952

IAS (Institute for Advanced Study Computer). Von Neumann's computer group at Princeton equipped their version of the EDSAC with a cathode ray storage system and parallel binary arithmetic. The result was a machine much faster than the acoustic delay line machines using serial arithmetic.

1947/1951

Whirlwind I. This machine was built by the Massachusetts Institute of Technology computer group; one of its notable developments was the coincident-current magnetic core memory.

1948/1951

UNIVAC (Universal Automatic Computer). This was the first large-scale commercially built machine. It was designed and constructed by the Eckert-Mauchly Computer Corporation (which lost its financial backing and was absorbed by the Remington-Rand Corporation). The first model was sold to the Bureau of the Census. At that time it was predicted that the total potential market for computers was perhaps six machines. "For almost five years . . . it was probably the best large-scale computer in use for data processing applications" [Rosen]. Not the least of the Eckert-Mauchly financial problems came from offering to sell its computers for a quarter of a million and then discovering that it cost a half million to produce them. As did Howard Aiken, some years earlier, Eckert and Mauchly first turned to IBM: "But word came uptown from galactic headquarters to brush them off" [Rodgers]. Then Remington-Rand stepped into the picture. "In the view of some, Rand was seeking to build his own version of the Watson image, but he continually recoiled from committing the capital essential to the task, the development, and the sales and distribution system. Over and over again, Remington-Rand had the opportunity in UNIVAC to take the lead in the world's newest and most promising industry. . . . Rand had repeatedly 'snatched defeat from the jaws of victory'" [Rodgers].

1948/1950

SWAC, SEAC (Standards' Western Automatic Computer and Standards' Eastern Automatic Computer). These machines were built by the Bureau of Standards when production lagged on the large-scale Hurricane computers which the Bureau ordered in 1948 from the Raytheon Corporation. The machines were small but quite fast. SEAC was the first stored-program machine to operate in the United States.

1948/1953

RAYDAC. The Raytheon Corporation built this large-scale computer of good design—as of 1948—which was already obsolete by the time it was completed, five years later. Raytheon unloaded its computer division onto the Honeywell Corporation in 1955.

1950/1953

DATATRON. The Electro-Data Corporation (which was spun off the Consolidated Engineering Corporation and later absorbed by the Burroughs Corporation) built this small but agile machine which was the first commercial computer to feature hardware index registers.

1951/1954

IBM 650. A fast drum, card-oriented machine represented IBM's entry into the medium scale computer field. Its initial design, which relied upon only card input and card output, would seem to have placed it at a disadvantage with respect to other machines (such as the Datatron) which had on-line printers and typewriters and magnetic tape auxiliary storage. But IBM sold more than a thousand of these machines. Later versions of the model had a large drum and sixty words of core storage.

1952/1956

BIZMAC. This large-scale computer, produced by RCA, was already obsolete when completed. "Perhaps the most important reason for this was RCA's inability to recognize the tempo of development in the computer industry" [Rosen].

1954/1957

NCR 304. National Cash Register (jointly with General Electric) produced this transistorized machine, signalling the end of the vacuum tube era for computers. (This machine, however, was too limited, too slow, and a commercial failure.)

1956/1960

Transac S-2000. In 1954 the Philco Corporation brought the state of development of the surface barrier transistors to the point where they could be used to produce very fast computer switching. Philco felt that its development of the technology gave it an advanced position in the computer industry and the S-2000 was the machine which it felt would exploit its advantage. "Although Philco had a head start, it lacked sufficient momentum. By the standards of the computer industry the Philco computer effort was small and poorly financed, and Philco was not ready to undertake the expansion that would have been necessary for a large penetration of the computer market" [Rosen]. By the time (1963) Philco was placing suitably modified versions of this machine on the market, the technology of the peripheral equipment had lapsed behind that of the computer itself. Philco's financial position had lapsed even more, and Philco was merged into the Ford Motor Company and thereby submerged.

1954/1958

IBM 709. The last of the big vacuum tube machines. Within a year of delivery, IBM had a faster, more powerful transistorized version of the same machine (the 7090 alias the 709TX) which was intended for delivery to the Ballistic Missile Early Warning System. The transistorized version was five times faster than the vacuum tube version. The first 7090's were delivered in late 1959 to the government and clearly rendered the 709 obsolete, placing IBM in the awkward position of having to write off a machine which it had just begun to deliver.

1955/1960

LARC. Remington-Rand Univac produced this one-of-a-kind "super" computer for the Atomic Energy Commission's Livermore Laboratory (run by the University of California). The machine had a four-microsecond cycle time and three computing units (two for calculation and one for input/output control) all operating in parallel. The machine itself represented a quite powerful design but ". . . the designers placed perhaps too much faith in the ability of the systems programmers to produce optimum performance in a very complicated hardware system" [Rosen].

1955/1961

STRETCH. IBM produced this machine as another one-of-a-kind super for the AEC Los Alamos Laboratory. The announced intent when the machine was designed was to produce a computer one hundred times faster than the currently offered commercial product (the 704). Its intended 0.5 microsecond memory and look-ahead instruction unit, together with an interleaved memory, seemed to embody a formidable design, but the machine turned out to be ". . . one of IBM's more memorable failures. . . Priced at $13,500,000, the STRETCH was designed to dwarf everything in size and power, and its very projection caused the stock of Control Data Corporation, which had set its sights on the market for massive computers in the scientific field, to sink badly" [Rodgers]. The commercial version of STRETCH was the 7030, for which IBM had a number of orders. But in 1961 IBM announced that the model had failed to meet its specifications. It was soon thereafter withdrawn from the product line. The 7030 was succeeded by the 7090 ("the most successful large scale computer any company has marketed" [Rosen]).

1960/1964

CDC 6600. Control Data Corporation produced this large-scale machine which turned out to be more than three times as fast as STRETCH. ("The STRETCH program failed at a cost of more than twenty million dollars, still leaving IBM with a near monopoly in most of the market, but opening the door for Control Data Corporation and its unduplicated 6600 computer, an eight million dollar installation in this highly sophisticated field" [Rodgers]. The 6600 had multiple arithmetic and logic units, which could be used in parallel, and ten peripheral processors (small computers toward which the central processor acted as slave), which monitored the calculations, input/output, and time-sharing.

1961/1965

System/360. IBM's intention in designing the 360 series was to produce a set of models spanning the power spectrum which, in a sense, would be uniformly programmable, and which would offer the computing power of the preceding generation of computers but at much less cost. No effort was made to make the series directly compatible with any preceding series (although the 360 series could be microprogrammed to simulate corresponding preceding models—a performance-degrading process). The new system was both word- and character-oriented, with every eight-bit byte directly addressable. Although a binary machine, it used hexadecimal floating-point and binary-coded decimal arithmetic. It relied upon hybrid circuitry rather than the newly developing monolithic integrated circuitry.

The exorcism of its old models and redesigning for the new 360 were of Homeric dimensions*. ". . . IBM spent nearly as much money to develop, redesign, program, and systematize its full line of computers [in the 360 series] as its gross sales of $5,345,000,000 in 1967. By dumping in staggering amounts of capital, far more than any combination of competing companies could or would commit, and by striding into the market armed with systems and equipment distinguished by all of the advanced design and compatibility technology the company could develop, imitate, or buy, IBM could keep most of the market to itself" [Rodgers].†

---

* T. A. Wise, "IBM's $5,000,000,000 gamble." *Fortune* **76** (Sept., Oct., 1966), 118; 138.
† From the book *Think, A Biography of the Watsons and IBM.* Copyright © 1969 by William Rodgers. Reprinted with permission of Stein and Day/Publishers.

1968/1971

B700 series. The Burroughs Corporation has designed a series of three machines (B5700, B6700, B7700). The most powerful of these is probably typical of the advanced commercial computers currently being produced; its main memory consists of six million bytes and has a cycle time of 1.5 microseconds, and its central processor unit has a cycle time of 62 nanoseconds.

1967/1971

CDC 7600 (and its late modification, the Cyber 70). Control Data's most powerful current system which has a 1.7 microsecond cycle time for its 256,000 words of main memory, and a central processor cycle time of 28 nanoseconds.

1967/1971

System 370. IBM's new series in which the most powerful model has a main memory with a 2.1 microsecond cycle time and an 80 nanosecond central processor cycle time.

1967/1971

ILLIAC IV. The current version of a "super" was designed at the University of Illinois and assembled by Burroughs. It consists of 64 sub-computers which operate in parallel. Computation takes place according to a sequence of instructions, but each instruction can be executed in the various sub-computers simultaneously (on different data). The memory cycle time is 350 nanoseconds. While each sub-computer has its own 2000 (64–bit) words of memory, there is a back-up disc memory of about 14 million words with an access time of 20 milliseconds but a transfer rate of a half billion bits per second. The machine has a further auxiliary memory that uses a laser beam as part of its read/write mechanism.*

---

* Slotnick, D. L. The fastest computer. *Scientific American* **224** (Feb., 1971), 76. Also, G. H. Barnes *et al*; The ILLIAC IV Computer. *IEEE Transactions C-17*, **8** (1968), 746–757.

The $ 30,000,000 cost of the machine was subsidized by the Advanced Research Projects Agency (Department of Defense).

REFERENCES

Bell, C. G. and Allen Newell, (1971), *Computer Structures: Readings and Examples*, New York: McGraw-Hill. (This is a massive presentation of various papers detailing the structure of many commercial computers; while the papers are drawn from a variety of sources and tend to be uneven in both style and intent, the editors supply some unifying connotation. The result is a deep and comprehensive view of the evolution of computer structure and a detailed anatomy for many specific machines.)

Rodgers, W. (1969), *THINK: A Biography of the Watsons and IBM*. New York: Stein & Day. (Rodgers gives a fascinating and provocative study of the evolution of the world's largest computer manufacturer and the concomitant growth of IBM's political power.)

Rosen, S. (1969), Electronic computers: a historical survey, *Computing Surveys* 1, 7–36.

The influence of American technology upon computer developments in Western Europe is partially treated in Rodgers' book. For a corresponding view of Soviet technology and its influence upon computer developments in Eastern Europe, the following two references are of interest.

Berenyi, I. (1970), Computers in Eastern Europe, *Scientific American* 222, 102–108.

Boehm, B. (1971), Current Soviet Computing, *Soviet Cybernetics Review* 1, 3–18.

5   The Golden Bit

In every cycle there is some industry whose stocks do not just rise; they go up 500, 700 percent. In the early sixties, these were the airlines: Northwest, Braniff, Delta, all went up 600, 800 percent. You don't have to hit a play like that more than once or twice in a lifetime. Figure it out.

... Back in the fifties ... the Russians put up a Sputnik and Joe Alsop discovered the missile gap, and all of a sudden any company that could make an instrument or components for a computer or an exotic fuel was a lovely, nubile thing.

When I think of those stocks now they are like the faces of girls we once took to football weekends. General Transistor, where are you now?*

'Adam Smith'

• •

The computer industry can be roughly segmented into five subdivisions: computer systems, peripherals and subsystems, supplies and accessories, software, and leasing. To watch the performance, on the stock market, of one of these segments is to know them all. For example, Fig. 1. (taken from *Computerworld*, June 10, 1970) shows the average stock prices for the five segments, all showing surprising synchronization as they take the toboggan ride down during the first half of 1970.

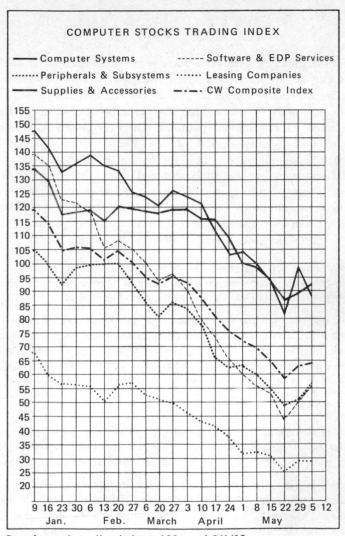

Base for each trading index: 100 as of 3/1/68

FIGURE 1 A study in synchronization: five segments of the computer industry during a notable quarter in their history, the first part of 1970. (From *Computerworld*, June 10, 1970.) Copyright by *Computerworld*, Newton, Mass. Reproduced by permission.

During the nineteen sixties the pace, vigor, and expansion of the computer industry gave it a golden glow. In the minds of investors and traders alike, the prospective market for data processing products seemed a thing of limitless promise—even though the war in Southeast Asia gave clear-cut evidence of an ominous pathology in government, from which a damaged economy must inevitably follow. The period 1969/1970 showed that even the strongest element—the computer industry—of the commercial spectrum can be badly dimmed when the economy is sick. Figure 1 shows what happened on the average, when the Big Board tilted and the prices slid down, but the kinetics of the individual member can be fairly understood from the neat characterization of the day (September 27, 1966) "they red-dogged Motorola," by 'Adam Smith'.

"They're out," Charley says. "They can't go to the Fed because the Fed will slam the window on their fingers if they look at their loans, so they have been scrambling around Europe sopping up Eurodollars."

If you understand what Charley said, fine, and if you don't, it doesn't have much to do with Motorola except that it sets a nice, dark, ominous atmosphere. Money is tight and Wall Street doesn't like the Vietnam war at all. Then a fellow we both know comes by and says Motorola is getting red-dogged down on the floor of the Exchange. Already there is a little crowd around the Dow-Jones broad tape in the anteroom where the carpet is worn.

Meanwhile, a couple of blocks away at 15 William Street the boys are spilling what is left of the tuna fish in order to get to the phones. All this from a speech by Mr. Robert W. Galvin from Franklin Park, Illinois.

Mr. Galvin is chairman of the board of Motorola, one of the flyers of the time, and he is addressing the sage and august New York Society of Security Analysts. Motorola, as you know, makes color TV sets, and that's growth, and semiconductors, and that's growth, and two-way radios, and that's growth. Growth, growth, growth.

Six months ago all this growth is worth $234 a share. On September 27 it's worth $140. A bad gassing, but how much worse can things be? They've going to earn $8 a share. It says so in Standard & Poor's. Business, Mr. Galvin says, is so good, it's bad. They have all the orders they can handle, they just have trouble producing the goods—shortages here, labor problems there. They can sell all the color TVs they can make, they just can't make them fast enough. Earnings will be up—but to $5.50, $6 on the outside. Everything else is rosy.

The sage and august analysts look at each other for a moment: $6? $6? What happened to the other $2?

Then it's like the end of the White House news conference, except nobody has even said, "Thank you, Mr. President." They're all running for the phones. Except they are security analysts, not newsmen, so they use the Olympic heel-and-toe walk instead of the outright sprint. There is a question-and-answer period, but Mr. Galvin's audience has been depleted.

. . . We stand there watching the tape, and there goes MOT, 137, 136, oof, 134. Big blocks are appearing.

. . . Now down on the floor the pressure is on the specialist. He is standing there on the floor at Post 18, his Hippocratic oath bidding him make an orderly market in Motorola, and suddenly there he is, like an adolescent fantasy, a quarterback in Yankee Stadium with the crowd roaring. Only it's the wrong dream. The crowd is roaring because all his receivers are covered, his defense has evaporated, and the red-dog is on:

two tons of beef descending on him, tackles grunting and linebackers growling *Killll*. Nothing to do but buckle, eat the ball, and hope you're still alive when they stop blowing the whistle.

Guys are bearing down on the specialist and he can tell that if he bends over in a reflex from the first chunk of Motorola that hits him in the stomach, they will hit him over the head with the rest. That's not an orderly market.

So they blow the whistle. No more trading in Motorola.

. . . At 3:29 the specialist reopened Motorola, just as the bell rang. That's like a boxer that manages to get on one knee just as the referee counts ten. Motorola reopened and closed at 119, down 19 on the day. In the market-place it was worth $114 million less at 3:30 than it was at 10:00 AM, and, say, $684 million less than it had been a few months before. And it was the same company, more or less, and this year is better than last year and next will be better than this year.

Despite the importance of semiconductors to the computer industry, Motorola might be said to be on the edge of the boundary of the industry. The Control Data Corporation, on the other hand, is solidly in the interior. CDC was formed in 1957 by a group who left Remington-Rand, armed with a good design for a transistorized computer and excellent prospects in the market. Their first machine, the 1604, was ready by 1960 and sold well to universities and some government agencies. A more powerful model, the 3600, was ready by 1963, and within a year later, the even more powerful 6000 series was being readied for sale. By 1966 CDC had a large piece of the market for big computer systems. The value of CDC stock climbed from $25, at the end of 1966, to $160, during 1967, and swung between $125 and $150 during most of 1968 and 1969.

During 1969 the money situation tightened ominously and buyers for large-scale computer systems tended to cancel orders or to request postponement of deliveries. Just as in the case of Motorola, three years earlier, CDC's troubles began with its earnings report at the end of September: third quarter profits, at 83¢ per share, were up 17 percent over the year before but somewhat lower than the expected dollar per share. Two blocks, amounting to 228,000 shares, were dumped at $140 per share, more than five points under the close of the preceding day. By the end of the trading session that day, CDC had dropped another fifteen points. By the end of the week the stock was down to $116.

The Federal Reserve Board severely administered a tight money policy through 1969 and 1970—until shortly before the elections—as part of a strategy of trying to contain a steadily increasing inflation. During that period, Control Data stock drifted down to a low, in summer 1970, of about $30.

Shortly before the elections, 1970, the Federal Reserve Board, in response perhaps to some mystic incantation, reversed its policy and began feeding currency into the economy at a sizable rate. The effect on the computer stocks was a sudden and dizzying climb. IBM went from $230 to $310, CDC went from $32 to $54, Burroughs from $87 to $126.*

---

* In the glow of this economic resonance, Robert W. Sarnoff, then chairman and president of RCA Corporation, announced on September 15, 1970, that his company was introducing a new line of computers which was intended to make RCA second only to IBM as a major computer manufacturer. But a year later (on September 17, 1971), Mr. Sarnoff announced that RCA had decided to drop

Irrespective of what was to come later, the spurt up continued until the beginning of October, when the Administration gave the details of what had been heralded as a "bold new peace plan" for Southeast Asia. The sage and august analysts mulled over the details: bold? new? The climb upward snapped to a standstill and for several months stock prices wavered erratically. But the Federal Reserve was now dedicated to flooding the economy with money,* and by Spring 1971 interest rates were falling toward normal levels and stock prices were generally floating higher.

It might be said that Control Data was a particularly vulnerable company, given the state of the economy 1969/1970, since it dealt with large-scale machines and lacked the financial strength to lease (as did IBM) rather than sell, when buyers evaporated from the market. According to this view, producers of mini-computers should have been a lot better off than was CDC. (In fact, almost everyone was better off than CDC.)

The biggest American producer of mini-computers is the Digital Equipment Company. A mini-computer is a machine that costs anywhere from a few thousand to perhaps $200,000. (The price could be pushed up to $500,000 by embedding the computer in a big enough system.) DEC produces a variety of small machines which span this price spectrum. When the economy is slack and interest rates are edging up toward 10 percent, it is reasonable to suppose that an institution or corporation in need of in-house computing power might hesitate to buy a system in the $2,000,000 to $5,000,000 range, yet be willing to go one-tenth that

---

out of the competition and would write-off the operation in the same year. The *Wall Street Journal* estimated that the loss, before taxes, might approach $500 million and thus make it the most memorable incident in the history of commercial *contre-temps*.

* H. E. Heinemann, in the *New York Times* of June 6, 1971, reported that the rate of increase in the money supply was the largest since 1950, and he quoted the *Monthly Economic Letter* of the First National City Bank as saying that the Federal Reserve Board was "in imminent danger of putting the economy back on the roller coaster." (There may be those, among Mr. Heinemann's readers, who, having seen IBM (over the preceding six weeks) drop from about 360 to about 310, felt that the economy had never really left the roller coaster.)

cost. So what did DEC do while CDC was probing for new depths during 1969/1970? DEC did some probing of its own. DEC started off in 1966 at about $10 per share, climbed fairly steadily until it reached a peak of about $120 per share in February 1970, and then took the roller coaster down to about $50 per share. (Thereafter it performed some interesting oscillations between $50 and $80 per share.)

It might be claimed that, while computer manufacturers (mini- or otherwise) could not be expected to do much better than did CDC or DEC (unless they had large reserves of capital as does IBM), one might expect that the situation would be somewhat less difficult for the companies that produce the peripheral equipment—tape drives, disc drives, printers, readers, teletypes—for computers. Since many computer installations tend to be I/O bound (since most computing takes place much, much faster than the linked input/output), any advances in the technology of the devices or the materials that would increase I/O efficiency are quite valuable. One of the more notable companies in this area of the industry is Memorex. Memorex started off in 1965 at about $10 per share and climbed fairly steadily to a peak of about $170 per share by November 1969. But the record of Memorex on the New York Stock Exchange, thereafter, is curiously erratic. With respect to one of its breathtaking descents, Richard Ney, in his caustic criticism* of the irregularities of specialists handling certain stocks on the floor of the NYSE, put it:

> And who, on February 4, 1970, opened Memorex 29 points lower than its previous closing price?

(Ney gives the answer in full and devastating detail.) That particular plunge took Memorex down to about $110, a low from which it feebly undertook to recover during the next three weeks, managing briefly to reach about $130 per share before taking the long ride down. By the end of summer, 1970, Memorex had dipped to $45 per share. (Its behavior since then has been one of the most spectacularly oscillatory on the Big Board.)

---

* From *The Wall Street Jungle*. Copyright © 1970 by Richard Ney. Reprinted by permission of Grove Press, Inc.

And what about the giant, IBM, with a current annual gross of about $7 billion? In January 1970, IBM stock had a relative peak of about $380 per share. Then, along with its lesser competitors, IBM took the ride down, and by summer hit a low of about $240 per share. The economic picture had grayed some of IBM's luster but, across the computer industry generally, it was among those that suffered the least relative loss. After the Federal Reserve Board switched to a loose money policy in Fall 1970, IBM stock climbed fairly steadily and by Spring 1971 had almost attained its previous peak.

A corollary to the barren economy of 1969/1970 was its effect upon one of the new thrusts of the computer industry: time-sharing. The concept of a computer utility implies not merely that institutions need not maintain an in-house computer but that any individuals who can buy or lease a terminal (and of course pay for their time slice) can access a powerful computer system just as if it were their own. But a strong and reliable time-sharing system is also a valuable in-house form of computer installation for institutions with large numbers of people who may need to access a computer at the same time and whose time and talent are badly wasted with the typical two-to-ten hour turn-around times of conventional computer installations. So the construction of a computer system appropriately designed for time-sharing seems to represent one of the last rich veins of computer ore that the major computer manufacturers have yet to sink a pick into.

The prospects of commercial exploitation of the time-share market led to the formation, during 1968/1969, of a number of new companies. Of these, three sprang up from the once-fertile industrial turf of golden California: the Mascor Corporation, the Berkeley Computer Corporation, and Computer Operations, Inc. There is a tenuous but discernible relation among their origins and a curious parallelism in their demise.

Early in the nineteen sixties the Army, through its Advanced Research Projects Agency (ARPA), funded a time-sharing research and development effort by a small group of electrical engineers at the University of California, Berkeley. The result was Project Genie, which created a small but facile time-share system built around a modified version of a computer—the 930—built by Scientific Data Systems. (SDS was later to

be absorbed by the Xerox Corporation and become Xerox Data Systems.)
SDS, in turn, then began production and marketing of the time-share
model, calling it the 940. In late 1968 the research group at the University formed themselves into an independent company, called the Berkeley
Computer Corporation, with the intent of constructing and operating a
time-share system capable of supplying remote access for as many as
500 simultaneous users of the system.

The construction of a new large-scale computer is a multi-million dollar
endeavor, and when the construction is performed by a company which
itself is new, the initial hurdle is collecting adequate financial support.
In the case of BCC, the intent was initially to construct a pair of machines
and to market the time-share capability which they would embody, and
thereafter to produce further machines and market them. Of course,
designing a new machine implies designing the software to implement its
service. BCC's estimate of its financial needs for all of this was about
$13 million. Given the meager money market, BCC was able to find only
two major investors—Data Processing Financial & General Corporation*
and the University of California†—and was able to obtain only one
quarter of its projected needs. By the beginning of Spring 1971, BCC
had a nearly complete computer, nearly adequate software, and no money.
The original investors declined to supply further support, and BCC
found itself suffering the Babbage syndrome.

The short happy life of the Mascor Corporation exhibits some sharp
parallels to that of BCC. Mascor was formed in the middle of 1969 largely

---

* DPF is a company primarily engaged in leasing computer systems—mostl
IBM 360 systems—which, at the end of 1970 were valued at about $180 millior
The company's revenues during 1969/1970 apparently were such that it w;
compelled to sell or close down its eight data centers, with the single exception
BCC, in which it had invested about $2.3 million.

† In 1969, in response to the stated intentions of the Regents of the Univers
to impose stiff tuition fees, students pointed out that the University's $6
million investment portfolio was yielding a notably meager return and offe
some harsh evaluations of the University's ability to devise a profitable inve
ment strategy. UC then decided to sink a substantial portion of the portfolio i
"high risk" ventures—for which BCC unquestionably qualified.

by a group who had just left the IBM laboratory at Menlo Park, California, where they had been concerned with the design of advanced computer systems. The original intent of the Mascor people was, first, to quickly build a machine which would correspond to an improved version of the 940 computer (and so provide both a highly marketable machine and a system of particular interest to a particular time-share corporation which was viewed as a prospective financier); second, with the expected revenues derived from this initial production model, the Mascor people intended to build and market a large-scale computer system of advanced design.

When the dust had settled from initial attempts to obtain financing, the prospective support from the time-share corporation had failed to materialize, but Mascor had the backing of the J. H. Whitney Corporation and Electronic Memories and Magnetics Corporation. The initial support amounted to $1.5 million, which, according to Mascor's projections, would carry the company for a year and a half. The failure in the negotiations with the time-share company led Mascor to decide to sidestep the production of the initial smaller machine and instead go directly to the design of the large-scale advanced system. Completion of this latter system would require about $7 million, but Mascor proceeded on the assumption that when the initial design was complete, further financing would be obtainable. In particular, there was an understanding that EM&M would pick up forty percent of the further required support.

At the end of Mascor's subsidized year and a half of operations, the company arrived at just the point where it expected to be: The advanced system's architecture design was complete and part of the logic design was complete. To prospective financial backers, the company could offer a fairly exact picture of the system which it could build and market at a price of about $5 million. But the decline in the economy had in the meantime sealed Mascor's fate. Whereas in 1969, EM&M had shown a substantial profit, for fiscal 1970 the company declared a loss of about $14 million and an inability to provide further financing for Mascor. In the financial community generally, potential investors shrugged off Mascor as an insufficiently attractive risk: The three-to-four year turnaround in the investment looked too long and the prospects of such a small company's being able to market such a large system were dubious.

In December, 1970, Mascor folded. Its life and death was almost synchronized with that of Computer Operations, Inc., of Costa Mesa, California. Computer Operations envisioned a powerful time-share system which it called the Gemini. The current conventional usage of computers views them as collections of capabilities. (Arithmetic/logical operation of the central processors is one capability; information transfer from memory to memory is another capability; information transfer from memory to input/output processors is another capability, and so forth.) To maximize efficiency, all capabilities should be simultaneously in use, and this is more likely to be the case if a number of independent programs are simultaneously in the computer (giving each such program a chance to use any capabilities not currently required by other programs). For a computer to handle a reasonably large number of programs concurrently requires a rather large, fast memory—or at least what *appears* to the computer as a large, fast memory, a virtual memory. In the Gemini design, the virtual memory (which results from juggling information between a fast bulk memory and a very fast but smaller adjunct memory) is divided into segments, with each segment consisting of over a billion byte addresses.

By Summer, 1970, Computer Operations had completed the logic design and sufficient system architecture to permit simulation of the Gemini's operation (on another computer) and, accordingly, the validity of the design. But superior designs are not invulnerable to the Babbage syndrome, and the classic drama of the Analytical Engine is not a hard act to follow. In the financial low tide of 1970, Computer Operations sank with hardly a ripple. As for the Gemini, it remains an impressive machine —on the drawing board.

REFERENCES

Allen, B. (1969), Time sharing takes off, *Harvard Business Review* **47**, 128–136.

Brealey, R. A. (1969), *An Introduction to Risk and Return from Common Stocks*. MIT Press.

Burck, G. (1968), The computer industry's great expectations, *Fortune* **78**, 92–97.

Ney, R. (1970), *The Wall Street Jungle*. Grove Press.

'Adam Smith' (1967), *The Money Game*. Dell Publishing Co.

Stock Market Study: Hearings, Committee on Banking and Currency, United States Senate. Government Printing Office, 1955.

Swartz, E. S. (1971), *Overskill. The Decline of Technology in Modern Civilization*. Chicago: Quadrangle.

6 Games Computers Play

One of the major problems we face in the 1970s is that so many computers will be built in the next decade that there will be a shortage of data to feed them.

Prof. Heinrich Applebaum, director of the Computer Proliferation Center at Grogbottom, has voiced concern about the crisis and has urged a crash program to produce enough data to get our computers through the seventies. "We didn't realize," the professor told me, "that computers would absorb so much information in such a fast period of time. But if our figures are correct, every last bit of data in the world will have been fed into a machine by Jan. 12, 1976, and an information famine will follow, which could spread across the world."*

Art Buchwald,
"The great data famine"
Washington Post, 1969

. . . .

Perhaps the most dramatic use of computers is in real-time applications such as the get-the-man-on-the-moon type and the cardiac-intensive-care monitoring type. Real-time means that data, derived from an event, are fed to the computer as the event occurs, and the computational response to these data should be almost immediate for the purposes at hand. In the case of space vehicles, on trajectory, tracking data is fed continuously to the computer so that the correctness of the trajectory is

---

* Reprinted by permission of Art Buchwald.

constantly monitored, and corrections, when needed, are quickly computed; in coronary intensive care units which have been computerized, part of the responsibility for monitoring electrocardiograms—and for initiating certain therapeutic action, in the event of an incident—has been lodged with the computer.

The ability to conduct split-second monitoring over a long period of time is not particularly notable in humans. So the transfer of monitoring-tasks to machines seems a natural development. The application of machines to monitoring patients in intensive-care-units poses three particular problems, which are in fact present in almost every real-time application of computers: (1) there is the problem of back-up support in the event that the computer experiences a (hardware) failure; (2) there is the problem of testing program logic; and (3) there is the problem of program reliability. Manufacturers of computing equipment are producing machines which are more reliable than preceding versions—in part because the quality of components is increasing with refinements in technology, and in part because computers can be designed so that when the computer itself detects an internal hardware failure, it is able to automatically switch a replacement into play (sometimes). With respect to (2), although (for example) patients in a cardiac ICU are not likely to be particularly resistant to acting as trial runs for a computer program test; nevertheless, the usual practice is to program-test on (a) laboratory animals and (b) simulated cardiac conditions. Note that by verifying program logic we mean that the programmer must verify that the *strategy* which the program represents is correct. On the other hand, (3) refers to the problems of verifying that the program really contains what the programmer intended it to contain.

The use of computers in real-time applications might be viewed as having mixed effects, depending upon who is being viewed as the beneficiary. For example, in a large oil refinery small computers are being introduced to monitor and control the flows of components through the refinery. There is a complicated inter-play between rates of flow of different components and the temperature and pressure at which chemical reactions are to be conducted, if the production of the more valuable components is to be maximized. Before the advent of computer control, several hundred workers would be required to monitor meters and reset valves, always trying to maintain optimal flow and reaction rates. The computer cuts the number of workers who are required by a factor of 10. Two years ago, a large petroleum refinery—during a strike by refinery workers—discovered that it could run most operations under computer control with practically no human intervention. The result of this discovery was, of course, loss of employment for a large number of workers. Inasmuch as the mathematics which deals with optimization problems has sharpened during the last decade, computers are able to produce a degree of control the optimality of which cannot be matched by humans (usually).

The same considerations apply across industry generally. The best-paid jobs are those which deal with the most complicated and/or delicate problems. These are just the problems that the computer was intended for. When industry replaces its workers by a computer various social responsibilities may be forgotten: overtime, social security, medical insurance ... The jobs for which the computer would be inappropriate would be just those which are too minor or trivial: The logic of commercial enterprise appears to dictate that these will be the jobs still available to humans as computers become more prevalent.*

One might ask: Is there *any* area of human endeavor in which the computer has not yet proved to be superior? A more intriguing question is: Is there any area in which the computer *cannot* be superior? The question is posed, thinking of the computer not so much as a *control* device but rather as a *think* device. For example, is there any principle which precludes a computer from playing chess in a fashion superior to that of the best human player? One way of approaching the latter question is to consider the information-holding capacities of the brain and the computer. Some approximate estimates are given by von Neumann† which provide an interesting comparison:

Assuming an acceptance rate of about 14 (digital pulses) per second on the part of the standard nervous system receptor (nerve cell) and using the usual figure of about 10^{10} such cells for the brain, and assuming a noneraseable memory, then in 60 years ($= 2 \cdot 10^9$ seconds), the brain ac-

---

* Walker, Charles R. *Technology, Industry & Man.* McGraw-Hill.
† Von Neumann, John, *The Computer and the Brain.* Yale U. Press.

cumulates about $3 \cdot 10^{20}$ bits of information. On the other hand, a computer with 60-bit words and one million words of memory can hold $6 \cdot 10^7$ bits of information. These figures suggest that man is potentially enormously superior to any computer of current conceivable design—as an information receptacle—even if the ability to recall all accepted information has an efficiency of only 0.001 percent.

Of course, information rates which relate only to *pertinent* information are microscopically smaller. If we consider the information flow of a rapid-transit chess game (one move per second, say), the input information from the board is at most 640 bits/sec. The human player offers a fairly high quality game with this transfer rate from the outside—we have no way of estimating what the *internal* information transfer rate is, for a rapid transit game—while the typical computer, operating at an internal transfer rate of about $3 \cdot 10^6$ bits/sec, requires that about $7 \cdot 10^8$ bits be processed per move (i.e., requires about four minutes per move). But increasing the speed of the computer (of current design) by a factor of 200 seems within the realm of practical possibility. (Computer memories based on photo, rather than magnetic, devices are claimed to be capable of increasing computer speeds by a factor of 10.)

So it seems likely that computers can be endowed with sufficient power to play good quality rapid-transit. Of course the question might be raised as to whether computers *should* be used as chess-players when they might be used for something more valuable—say practicing medicine. Can a computer equal a finely trained, keenly intuitive internist? A given disease has a certain collection of symptoms associated with it. A specific victim of the disease may have some subset of these symptoms. In a study* using statistics compiled by the Permanente Medical Group, one respiratory disease, with seven symptoms, was subjected to a computer analysis. The result was the distribution of patients with symptom-complexes. (A symptom-complex is just the subset of possible symptoms actually observed in a particular case.) There are $2^7 - 1 = 127$ nonempty subsets of seven symptoms, but no one would expect that *any* subset of the set of possible symptoms would be observed sooner or later (for a particular

---

* "A note on computer diagnosis," *IEEE Transactions on Bio-medical Engineering*, BME–11 (1964), 8–12.

disease); still the specialists were surprised to find that 44 distinct symptom-complexes were observed for a single sample (of several hundred patients) in the seven-symptom case.

If we assume an average of only 10 symptom-complexes for the approximately 5000 items in the materia medica, there are about 50,000 symptom-complexes that the ideal diagnostician should be able to differentiate. For those physicians that have not yet attained the ideal ability, it might be useful to have a computer-accessible data bank which, upon query, not only presents possible identifications of diseases corresponding to stated symptom-complexes, but also the recommended therapy and current references to the literature. The American Medical Association, well known for its aggressive political approach on social-medical questions, has yet to suggest either a self-sponsored or federal-sponsored medical data bank. (The Government, meanwhile, is wandering off in other directions in the use of data banks—as we shall see below.)

It might be asked whether, at this point, the technology is available that can cope with an information-retrieval problem of such scope. The answer is suggested by a notable study* of an information-retrieval system designed by the Stanford University Computer Center. In this case, the information stored in the system consisted of the contents of three star catalogues; and for accessing the information (both for retrieval and up-dating), a special and rather natural language was devised. The type of question-and-answer interplay that took place on the system is illustrated in Fig. 2. (In the figure, those lines beginning with a colon are queries from a user; the other lines are the computer's response.) The information was stored in the system (at Stanford), while querying was performed via terminals located at Northwestern University (Evanston, Illinois). The amount of information stored was of the order of 10 million bits.

How does this compare with the corresponding amount of information in the medical situation? A medical data bank might be expected to hold a minimum of 20,000 bits per disease, hence about 100 million bits altogether—only a factor of 10 larger than the amount involved in the Stanford study.

---

* Research Report Number II, September 1970. Scientific Information Networks: a case study. Jacques Vallee. Stanford University Computation Center.

```
        QUERY
FILE    IDENTIFICATION
:       A010
ACTION
:       SELECT
SELECTION RULES
:       Cluster CONTAINS Virgo END
```

24 RECORDS SELECTED
```
ACTION
:       RETAIN
ACTION
:       SN CONTAINS s END
```

1 RECORDS SELECTED
```
ACTION
:       DISPLAY SN Vs Cluster
```

```
SN          s 1922alpha
VS          1243
Cluster     Virgo
```

1 RECORDS SELECTED
```
ACTION
:       RELEASE
ACTION
:       CLUSTER CONTAINS Virgo AND SN DOES NOT CONTAIN s
        END
```

23 RECORDS SELECTED
```
ACTION
:       RETAIN
ACTION
:       Vs EXISTS END
```

19 RECORDS SELECTED
```
ACTION
:       Vs (< = 2000 AND > = 1000) END
```

FIGURE 2 On-line interrogation of an astronomical catalogue.

```
11 RECORDS SELECTED
ACTION
:      Sources (FIRST) CONTAINS "MT. Wilson" END
```

```
 1 RECORDS SELECTED
ACTION
:      DISPLAY SN Vs 12 b2 Sources END
```

SN	1901b
Vs	1617
12	271.15
b2	76.90

Sources 1 Ap.J., 88(1938),285–304– Contr.Mt.Wilson, 25 (1938)
No. 600
2 XIV Colloque Intern.Astrophys., Paris (1941), 186, 188.
3 Annales Observ. de Paris, 9 (1945) fasc. 1, 165–179.
4 Astronomie 55 (1941), 78, 106.
5 Astronomie 63 (1949), 68.
6 . . .

FIGURE 2 (cont.)

The excellence with which the computer serves as librarian depends critically upon the skill and understanding with which it is programmed. Inadequate programming efforts sometimes conceal the latent power of the librarian computer. For example, consider the view of Lewis Mumford:

The National Library of Medicine, in Bethesda, Maryland, has an information-retrieval service (MEDLARS) designed to index the medical literature in 2300 periodicals. This system has been in operation since 1963, and by 1968 half a million articles were in storage. To compare the results of a computerized search with those achieved in the conventional manner, two staff members of the Radcliffe Science Library, in England, compiled a list of references on the same subject, covering the period covered by the MEDLARS taped record. Though nine relevant references in MEDLARS were not discovered by the library staff, they did dig out thirteen relevant references not included in the MEDLARS tape. This confirmed the negative verdict of Y. Bar Hillel, a mathematical logician, in his "Language and Information" (1964). Alike on grounds of promptness and low cost and qualitative value, human agents were preferable to the automation.*

(There is a nice parallel between this little competition and Marchant's play "The Desk Set.") Mumford also recounts a recent space spectacular, to make his point. (While it is not pertinent to the computer-librarian context, it has some interest in its own right.)

An even more dramatic instance was provided by the Apollo 11 moon landing. At a critical moment in making the descent to the moon, the astronaut's computer repeatedly announced its inability to handle the data. In human terms, it panicked. As a consequence, the ground-control officers were for a moment on the point of aborting the mission. Fortunately they made the radical decision to close off part of the computer and let the astronauts alone manage the final stages of the landing.

While this incident may not make Mumford's point, the point† itself is well worth quoting:

In short, the efficiency and applicability of the computer depend upon the ability of its human employers quite literally to keep their own heads, ‡ not merely to scrutinize the programming but to reserve for themselves the right of ultimate decision. No automatic system can be intelligently run by automatons—or by people who dare not assert human intuition, human autonomy, human purpose.

---

* Lewis Mumford. "The Megamachine" in *The Myth of the Machine: The Pentagon of Power.* Harcourt Brace Jovanovich, Inc. Originally published in *New Yorker Magazine*, October 24, 1970. This excerpt and the two following are reprinted by permission.

† Apollo 13 provided an even more dramatic instance of the need to keep cool during a spatial crisis (and one in which a computer did not figure). The core of the crisis lay in the fact—in both cases—of astronauts being in critical danger. The Russians avoided this side issue by letting their computers handle the moonshot and keeping their astronauts safe on the ground.

‡ One is reminded of Mark Twain's remark: If you can keep your head when all about you are losing theirs, perhaps you haven't heard the news.

REFERENCES

Apter, M. J. (1970), *The Computer Simulation of Behavior*. London: Hutchinson & Co.

Banerji, R. B. (1969), *The Theory of Problem-solving: An Approach to Artificial Intelligence*, New York: American Elsevier.

Bargellini, P. L. (1965), Considerations on man versus machines for space probing, *Advances in Computers* **6**, eds. F. L. Alt and M. Rubinoff, Academic Press.

Heiliger, E. M. and P. B. Henderson (1971), *Library Automation. Experience, Methodology, and Technology of the Library as an Information System*. New York: McGraw-Hill.

7 Playing the Game

One day last month two young amateur gamblers strode confidently into Reno's gaudy Palace Club. They were armed with a bankroll of $120 and a "scientific" theory cooked up between classes at the University of Chicago.

Tall, talkative Albert Hibbs, a graduate student in mathematics at Chicago, had devised the system on a bet with medical student Roy Walford. They took a term off from the university to try it out. It was a "progressive parlay" based on mathematical probability, some intricate slide rule calculations, and two assumptions: that any roulette wheel follows a pattern of its own, and that good or bad luck runs in streams. The key to the Hibbs/Walford approach: increase bets in streams of good luck, never increase or reduce them in times of bad luck.

. . . For four days the partners studied a Palace Club roulette wheel, jotting down the winning numbers and recording the machine's pattern. On the fifth day Hibbs & Walford selected No. 21 and made their first bet—a cautious 25¢. As their winnings mounted, the crowd of tourists, gamblers, divorce-seekers and hangers-on increased. So did the Hibbs/Walford bets, until $11 was riding on each spin . . . Hibbs and Walford spelled each other in eight-hour shifts. After 40 hours, when Hibbs & Walford had parlayed their $120 into $6000, the management changed the wheel heads . . .*

Time Magazine
December 1, 1947

. . . .

---

* Reprinted by permission from *Time*, The Weekly Newsmagazine; Copyright Time Inc., 1947.

The art of simulating games (and many probabilistic situations) is so simple on the computer, that even relatively inexperienced programmers have little trouble in constructing effective mockups. But since people are enormously more complicated than the games they play, it is not so easy to simulate the *players*. In a game like Nim or Tic-tac-toe there is an algorithm which realizes an optimal line of play: If a win is possible, from a given position, the algorithm for the optimal line (i.e., the strategy) automatically produces a win. But there are other games—chess and Go, for example—for which no winning strategy is known. For such games we may marvel at the skill of its master players while admitting their perplexity over the obscure intuitions by which they achieve their triumphs. Of course, when we say that no winning strategy is known, what we really mean is that a *practical* winning strategy is unknown. Given any game for which there are only finitely many plays, in principle all such plays could be enumerated and the existence of an optimal strategy could be decided. But if we consider applying this approach to chess, since there are usually about ten sensible possible moves in a given position, there are about 10^{60} corresponding variations to be explored for games of thirty moves. And a computer able to pursue a 30-move variation within 10^{-4} second would require about 1500 years to cull through all these games. Too long for practical competition.

Since there *are* chess-playing programs (which are surprisingly effective) and these cannot enumerate all possible variations, how do they style their strategy? Mostly by exploring possible variations to a depth of several moves and certain critical variations to a depth of a half dozen moves, assigning weights to these variations in accordance with some *ad hoc* valuation function, and then selecting that variation which maximizes the value of the valuation function. (If the optimal variation is not unique, then a selection may be made, among the optimal choices, at random.) There currently seems to be no adequate theory either for formulating appropriate valuation functions for these chess-playing programs or even for mimicking the mysterious and unarticulated intuitive evaluations of the chess masters. But, on the other hand, for games that *do* have algorithms for their play and in which the vexing perplexities of human thought processes do not intervene, the simulation-by-computer is rather easy.

We consider a simple example of game simulation and some FORTRAN programming that effects the simulation. Suppose that we wish to simulate play on a roulette wheel, say with a zero and a double-zero. We may as well start by numbering the slots from 1 to 38. We might consider two players, to be simulated as well, and we name these P and Q. We suppose that P and Q have rather simplistic lines of play: P bets always on even numbers, and Q bets always on number 31. (Let the zero be slot 37 and the double-zero be slot 38.)

We need some notation for the variables involved in the simulation. We let NP be the size of P's purse and NQ be the size of Q's purse. We let T be the number of spins that have occurred since the beginning of the simulation. We let K be the number of the slot resulting from the current spin.

We consider a particular case, say a simulation of 200 spins, in which P starts with a purse of 50, and Q starts with a purse of 120. Then an informal program for the simulation is:

1. Define P's purse and Q's purse and set T to zero.
2. Spin the wheel; get a random value for K ($1 \leqq K \leqq 38$).
3. Check whether P loses; if not, increment NP and go to 5.
4. Decrement P's purse.
5. Check whether Q has won or lost; increment Q's purse by 36 for a win, decrement it by 1 for a loss.
6. Increment the tally of spins.
7. Print the current values of the number of spins and the two purses.
8. Check whether the tally of spins has reached 200; if so, stop; otherwise go to 2.

If we encode the informal program into a FORTRAN program, we get:

```
    INTEGER NP, NQ, T
  1 NP  =  50
    NQ  =  120
    T  =  0
  2 K  =  38 * RANF(0)  +  1
```

```
3 IF (K .EQ. 37 .OR. K .EQ. 38) GO TO 4
  J = MOD(K,2)
  IF (J .NE. 0) GO TO 4
  NP = NP + 1
  GO TO 5
4 NP = NP - 1
5 IF (NQ .EQ. 0) GO TO 6
  IF (K .EQ. 31) NQ = NQ + 36
  IF (K. NE. 31) NQ = NQ - 1
6 T = T + 1
7 PRINT 9, T, NP, NQ
8 IF (T .EQ. 200) STOP
  GO TO 2
9 FORMAT (3112)
  END
```

Running the above program yields the following results:

T	NP	NQ
1	49	119
2	50	118
3	49	117
4	48	116
5	47	152
6	48	151
⋮	⋮	⋮
111	47	146
12	46	182
13	47	181
⋮	⋮	⋮
39	49	155
40	48	191
41	49	190
⋮	⋮	⋮

99	35	132
100	36	131
101	35	167
.	.	.
.	.	.
.	.	.
181	33	87
182	32	123
.	.	.
.	.	.
.	.	.
200	30	105

In the above record we have included all the spins on which Q won. In the 200 spins, Q won just five times, or about once every 40 spins. (If the wheel is perfect, then, given a very large number of spins, Q should get a winning spin, on the average, once every 38 spins.) Notice that, even with some remarkable luck early in the game—Q is ahead by 71 on the 40th spin—Q's purse is badly dented after 200 spins. (P is even worse off.) In the end, the odds must finally cut down the players—the casinos are in business because they have a sure thing.

8 Computer Pretense: the simulation extended

Man is a gaming animal. He must always be trying to get the better in something or other.

Charles Lamb

I am sorry I have not learnt to play at cards. It is very useful in life: It generates kindness and consolidates society.

Samuel Johnson

. . . .

Two aspects of the preceding roulette simulation are worth considering. The first applies to any probabilistic simulation: The results of the simulation give only clues as to the nature of the situation being simulated; the clues take on greater significance only as the number of simulations increases to a statistically significant level. The second applies to the reliability of probabilistic simulations: The reliability depends in part upon statistical theory being used to interpret properly the results and in part upon the reliability of the numerical device used to generate random numbers. We consider this latter question first.

A sequence of calls to RANF produces a sequence of real numbers x which all satisfy $0 < x < 1$ and which tend to scatter fairly uniformly across the $[0,1]$ interval. This sequence of values of x is generated according to an algorithm, so of course each time the sequence is generated anew, the result is the very same sequence again. (There is a way to start anew with a different sequence, but that does not concern us here.) The question of whether a sequence which is generated by an algorithm (and hence, *ipso facto*, is not random) can nevertheless be regarded as "random" really comes down to: Does the sequence pass various subtle tests that mathematicians have devised to test for randomness? In the case RANF, it turns out that the generated sequence *does* pass many of these tests in an acceptable way. Accordingly, we hereafter take it for granted that RANF is a reliable "random" number generator and that we can expect meaningful results when we use it in simulations.

Now we come back to the first point—obtaining a large enough sample to yield statistically significant results. It is just here that the speed of the computer provides us with a matchless tool for analysis. In particular, most games of chance have such simple structure that they can be simulated in a statistically significant way by a computation lasting only a second or so in time.

> ". . . But before I finished with the computer, I'd worked out a basic strategy for beating blackjack. I had calculated all the probabilities of the complete deck. And, as I cased the cards, I could determine to the decimal point my chances of winning or losing on each hand. I'd played a million hands, which would have taken me a lifetime to do without the computer. The only thing I had no control over was the arrangement of the cards. But with my six thousand dollars I could buck the house and come out winners. I couldn't lose."*

So say Eddie Clark, in Sam Ross's novel, *The Fortune Machine*. Clark, a young high school drop-out, is a gifted programmer who has been seeking a winning strategy for blackjack that would take advantage of his total-recall memory. He finally works out such a strategy after some simulations on a 360/40—bootlegging the machine time from a computer-dating company for which he works. He goes to Vegas and tries his system for real, backed by his wealthy girl friend. (How does he meet the girl?—the good old data bank back at Computer March.)

---

* Sam Ross. *The Fortune Machine*. Delacorte Press, 1970. Reprinted by permission.

Does the strategy that worked on the 360/40 also work over the black-jack tables? After a few mis-starts, Clark finds that his procedure effectively piles up chips and electrifies pit bosses, horrifies casino owners, and dazzles show girls. Ross's novel is a tight fictional parallel to the actual domination of blackjack that resulted from an elaborate analysis of the game by several mathematicians* during the nineteen sixties.

Coming back to the Hibbs/Walford venture, the key to their winning strategy is an unbalanced roulette wheel, and the assumption that every actual wheel might very well be an unbalanced wheel. They watched a wheel for approximately 5000 spins before trying to decide whether the wheel was balanced or not. If we look at the result of the first 5000 spins of our simulated wheel, what sort of distribution turns up? We find that the distribution looks like:

1	131	20	132
2	130	21	123
3	138	22	127
4	141	23	128
5	119	24	128
6	121	25	145
7	133	26	125
8	109	27	122
9	154	28	144
10	118	29	133
11	148	30	151
12	142	31	127

---

* Edward O. Thorp, *Beat the Dealer*. Vintage Books, 1966.

Thorp published a winning strategy for blackjack in 1962, and (in the 1966, revised, edition of his book) credits several other mathematicians with important refinements of his strategy. Some of these announced their results at the Fall Joint Computer Conference of 1963—held in Las Vegas—and then went out on the town and reproved the theory over the tables.

Blackjack seems to be one of the few games of chance in which a winning strategy is possible. American casinos use an effective counter-measure against winners: The casinos simply bar winners from further play.

13	122	32	133
14	126	33	130
15	142	34	118
16	132	35	141
17	112	36	148
18	144	37	130
19	131	38	122

The slot that turned up the largest number of times is 9 with 154 wins. For a balanced wheel the expected number of wins is just the probability of a win times the number of spins, which is $5000/38 = 132$ approximately. Since 154 is substantially larger than 132, it might appear that the wheel is unbalanced in favor of slot 9. But there are two reasons for considering this appearance to be misleading. First, if slot 9 really turned up much more frequently than expected because of a wheel unbalance, we would expect the neighboring slots 8 and 10 also to turn up more frequently than expected; but slot 8 with a score of 109, and slot 10 with a score of 118, have notably *low* scores. Second, if we apply one of the statistician's favorite tests—the chi-square test*—to slot 9's score under the assumption that all slots have equal probability to win, we find that a score of 154 is not too unreasonable. In other words, Hibbs and Walford would presumably have rejected a wheel with the above distribution for 5000 spins.

For comparison we shall simulate an unbalanced wheel. In this case, instead of the probability of a slot (scoring a win) being constant, around the wheel, the probability now corresponds to a function that has the form

$$a + b \cdot \sin^2(\theta/2)$$

where a and b are constants, and θ is angular distance around the wheel $(0 \leq \theta \leq 2\pi)$. So, whereas the balanced wheel gives each slot a probability of 0.0263 $(= 1/38)$, the simulated unbalanced wheel gives each slot the probability of winning according to the following table.

---

* This, and similar tests, are well described in H. Cramér, *Mathematical Methods of Statistics*. Princeton, 1951.

Unbalanced Wheel Probability Distribution

1	.0191682	20	.0334633
2	.0194620	21	.0331695
3	.0199428	22	.0326888
4	.0205974	23	.0320342
5	.0214080	24	.0312236
6	.0223524	25	.0302792
7	.0234050	26	.0292266
8	.0245369	27	.0280947
9	.0257174	28	.0269142
10	.0269142	29	.0257174
11	.0280947	30	.0245369
12	.0292266	31	.0234050
13	.0302792	32	.0223524
14	.0312236	33	.0214080
15	.0320342	34	.0205974
16	.0326888	35	.0199428
17	.0331695	36	.0194620
18	.0334633	37	.0191682
19	.0335622	38	.0190694

Simulating 5000 spins on the unbalanced wheel gives the following scores:

1	96	20	163
2	97	21	161
3	91	22	161
4	116	23	153
5	120	24	173
6	112	25	138
7	105	26	150
8	114	27	142
9	116	28	157
10	134	29	131
11	141	30	124

12	145	31	113
13	169	32	111
14	152	33	90
15	155	34	120
16	174	35	108
17	161	36	103
18	164	37	88
19	163	38	89

Even a casual inspection of the scores suggests that the chances of winning, on some slot near 17 or on 17 itself, look rather good in comparison with slots near 1 (or 38). Further, the root mean square deviation (assuming a balanced wheel) is about 27, which is much too large: This again is in favor of a wheel behaving as the one above, being unbalanced.

Next we want to see what happens with a Hibbs/Walford mode of play on this unbalanced wheel. We may as well suppose that they choose number 17 as a likely bet, that they start with a purse of 100, and that they bet one unit per spin unless their purse increases to over 200, in which case they bet two units unless their purse is over 400, in which case they bet ten units.

The program to simulate this type of play is given below, where again we use P for the players' purse, T to tally the number of spins, and K for the number turning up at any spin. And as before, we fix the game to end after 5000 spins if the player's purse has not already been reduced to zero.

1. Set P to 100, and set T to zero.
2. Spin the wheel for the current value of K.
3. If K is not 17, then decrement the purse P by 1 if P < 200, decrement the purse by 2 if 200 < P < 400, and decrement the purse by 10 if P ≥ 400; after decrementing, go to 5.
4. If K = 17, then increment the purse by 36 times the amount of the bet.
5. Check whether the purse has been reduced to zero; if so, stop.
6. Increment the tally T by 1 and if T > 5000, then stop.
7. Go to 2.

A FORTRAN encoding for this program is given below. In the encoding, we use a function called SPIN to produce the value of K for the unbalanced wheel. (Our print-out procedure has not been specified and has been chosen to yield only an outline of the action.)

```
      INTEGER P, T, SPIN
1  P = 100
   T = 0
2  K = SPIN(T)
3  IF (K .EQ. 17) GO TO 4
   IF (P.LT. 200) P = P − 1
   IF (P.GE. 200 .AND. P .LT. 400) P = P + 72
   IF (P.GE. 400) P = P − 10
   GO TO 5
4  IF (P .GE. 400) P = P + 360
   IF (P .GE. 200 .AND. P .LT. 400) P = P + 72
   IF (P .LT. 200) P = P + 36
5  IF (P .EQ. 0) STOP
6  T = T + 1
   IF (T .GT. 5000) STOP
7  IF (MOD(T,100) .EQ. 0) PRINT 8, T, P
   CO TO 2
8  FORMAT (2I14)
   END
```

Note that the above program simulates both the player and the croupier (the choice of the size of the bet, for the former, and the collection of bets on losses and the payoff for wins, for the latter). The simulation of the probabilistic part of the play is masked by the instruction

```
2 K = SPIN(T)
```

which we shall spell out below. First, we remark that the print-out decision at instruction 7 (which produces a printout of the current situation just in case the remainder, upon the division of T by 100, is zero) is somewhat arbitrary. (Moreover, a mildly more complicated version of the above program would run faster.)

The course of the simulated play then looks like:

T	P	T	P
1	99	2600	189
2	98	2700	197
.	.	2800	258
:	:	2900	280
100	111	3000	748
200	159	3100	1228
300	272	3200	2078
400	413	3300	1448
500	345	3400	2298
600	172	3500	2408
700	163	3600	2888
800	174	3700	2628
900	193	3800	3478
1000	304	3900	3588
1100	151	4000	3698
1200	88	4100	3438
1300	136	4200	2438
1400	147	4300	2178
1500	192	4400	2288
1600	187	4500	2398
1700	192	4600	2878
1800	92	4700	3728
1900	196	4800	4208
2000	133	4900	4318
2100	181	5000	4428
2200	155		
2300	166		
2400	140		
2500	77		

One somewhat surprising element in the course of play is the indication (at 2500 spins) that the player came close to being wiped out after so many spins. Not so surprising are the big fluctuations that occur late in the game (when the bet is increased to 10 per spin). Musing over this table, it is easy to see how people become fascinated with the theory of probability.

The above simulation of a 5000 spin game requires 3 seconds on the CDC 6400. It corresponds to one full week of play in the casino.

The FORTRAN code which generates the probability distribution for the slots of the unbalanced wheel is obtained by adding a small perturbation (of the form indicated above) to the probability distribution for the balanced wheel, and then renormalizing the perturbed values (so that they sum to unity).

```
  PI = 4 * ATAN (1.0)
  PROB = 1.0/38.0

  SUM = O
  DO 2 J = 1, 38
  P(J) = PROB + 0.02 *SIN(J*PI/38)**2
2 SUM = SUM + P (J)

  DO 3 J = 1, 38
3 P (J) = P (J) / SUM
```

The values P(J) form the perturbed probability distribution for the unbalanced wheel. But in using this distribution it is more convenient to use the *cumulative* probability distribution $Q(J) = P(1) + P(2) + \cdots + P(J)$.

```
  Q(1) = P(1)
  DO 4 J = 2, 38
4 Q(J) = P(J) + Q(J-1)
```

Once the Q(J) have been defined, the function SPIN returns the random slot number by use of the code:

```
5 Y = RANF (0)
  DO 6 J = 1, 38
  IF (Y .GT. Q(J)) GO TO 6
  SPIN = J
  RETURN
6 CONTINUE
```

If we put it all together, we get:

```
INTEGER FUNCTION SPIN (N)
REAL P(38), Q(38)
IF (N .GT. 0) GO TO 5
PI = 4 *ATAN(1.0)
PROB = 1.0 / 38.0

SUM = 0.
DO 2 J = 1, 38
P(J) = PROB + 0.02 *SIN(J*PI/38.0)**2
2 SUM = SUM + P(J)
DO 3 J = 1, 38
3 P(J) = P(J) / SUM
Q(1) = P(1)
DO 4 J = 2, 38
4 Q(J) = P(J) + Q(J-1)
5 Y = RANF(0)
DO 6 J = 1, 38
IF (Y .GT. Q(J)) GO TO 6
SPIN = J
RETURN
6 CONTINUE

RETURN
END
```

As the above example suggests, if there is an algorithm for playing a game, then it is generally straightforward to simulate plays of the game that correspond to applications of the strategy. But, as we observed earlier, there are games such as chess for which no algorithm for winning is known. In such a case, of course, algorithms can still be devised for playing-by-computer but the efficacy of such algorithms depends largely upon the articulation of the best human intuition that has been applied to the game. A tentative analysis of how a computer approach to chess might be formulated was given by Claude Shannon in 1950*. Two specific realizations of chess-playing programs were given a chance to play against each other in the U.S.A.-U.S.S.R. computer chess match that took place in 1966–1967.

The contestants in the U.S.A.-U.S.S.R. match were a program developed in John McCarthy's Artificial Intelligence project at Stanford University and a program developed at the Siberian Branch of the U.S.S.R. Academy of Sciences. The latter program was written by a Russian mathematician, V. Butenko, in accordance with a strategy devised by the former world chess champion, M. M. Botvinnik (who held the title from 1948 until 1963, except for a two-year break). The Russian program won the four-game match by a score of 3–1. One of the games from the match is given below. It appears, along with some caustic annotations, in a provocative little book by Botvinnik†. White is played by the Moscow program and Black by the Stanford program.

	W	B
1.	P — K4	P — K4
2.	N — KB3	N — QB3
3.	N — QB3	B — B4
4.	N × P	N × N
5.	P — Q4	B — Q3
6.	P × N	B × P
7.	P — B4	B × N ch
8.	P × B	N — B3
9.	P — K5	N — K5
10.	Q — Q3	N — B4
11.	Q — Q5	N — K3
12.	P — B5	N — N4

---

* Shannon, C. Programming a computer for playing chess, *Philosophical Magazine* **41** (1950). Reprinted in *The World of Mathematics*, Vol. 4, ed. J. R. Newman, Simon & Shuster, New York, 1962.

† Botvinnik, M. M. *Algoritm igry v shakmaty*, [An algorithm for the game of chess]. Translated as *Computers, Chess and Long-Range Planning*, by Arthur Brown, Springer-Verlag. 1970.

13. P − KR4	P − KB3
14. P × N	P × P (N4)
15. KR × P	R − Bl
16. R × P	P − B3
17. Q − Q6	R × P
18. R − N8 ch	R − Bl
19. Q × R mate	

In his remarks concerning these games, Botvinnik observed that both the Stanford and Moscow programs were relatively helpless in the endgame, and accordingly both sides had agreed to terminate any games after the fortieth move. (Since then, certain endgame variations have received further study from the Stanford artificial intelligence project*.) A more recently developed chess program†, developed by the artificial intelligence project at the Massachusetts Institute of Technology has won a class D trophy and has been made an honorary member of the United States Chess Federation. So it presumably enjoys a wider capability over the entire range of the game.

Whether any of these programs will deepen our understanding of chess remains to be seen. But they represent one facet of a captivating endeavor: the application of human intuition to the problem of human intuition—a problem which may be immeasurably more difficult than that of how to win at chess.

One might wonder whether, since computers can be set to playing chess on their own, can they also pursue autonomously a more significant game—mathematics? The answer seems to be: not yet. Hao Wang, in *A Survey of Mathematical Logic*, reported that his theorem-proving program was able to dispose of the more than two hundred theorems in the first five chapters of *Principia Mathematica* (of Whitehead and Russell) with less than three minutes of computing time; but as for a more serious

---

* Huberman, B. *A program to play chess endgames, Tech. Rep. CS 106*, Computer Science Dept., Stanford University, August 1968.

† Greenblatt, R. D., D. E. Eastlake, and S. D. Crocker. *The Greenblatt Chess Program*, Proceedings, AFIPS Fall Joint Computer Conference, 1967.

program, written to *find* theorems in the restricted predicate calculus: "The result was disappointing in so far as too few theorems were excluded [by the computer] as being trivial . . ." So far, the more sensible approach seems to be that described by a group at the Applied Logic Corporation, Princeton, who have constructed programs for theorem finding/proving in which the course of computation involves intervention of the mathematician; thus, at crucial points during the computation, the control of which way the pursuit should go, rests upon the mathematician's judgment—permitting the interjection of that elusive element, spontaneous insight, which has yet to be bred into our machines. Professor D. H. Lehmer, in his essay "Some high-speed logic," offers some non-trivial examples of theorem-proving, in the area of number theory, in which he generously cites the machine for its contribution*. The theorems in question are non-trivial—they state a truth about infinitely many cases—and they are proved by reducing the proof to the computation of a finite number of cases (which the computer is assigned to check, since the checking seems to be beyond the range of human patience). But, as Lehmer himself observes, the semantics of what constitutes theorem-proving hasn't been really formalized yet, so the legitimacy of any particular claim is a bit difficult to determine. As for the present case, we merely note that the machine was not listed as co-author of the published results†.

REFERENCES

Aleksander, I. (1970), Computers get more like human brains, *Elektronische Datenverarbeitung* **12**, 267–268.

---

* Lehmer, D. H. Some high-speed logic, *Proceedings of Symposia in Applied Mathematics*, Vol. 15: Experimental arithmetic, high speed computing and mathematics American Mathematical Society, 1963.

† Lehmer, D. H., Emma Lehmer, W. H. Mills and J. L. Selfridge. Machine proof of a theorem on cubic residues, *Mathematics of Computation* **16** (1962), 407–415.

Banerji, R. and M. D. Mesarovic (1970), *Theoretical Approaches to Non-numerical Problem Solving*. New York: Springer-Verlag.

Botvinnik, M. M. (1970), *Computers, Chess, and Long Range Planning*, translated from the Russian by Arthur Brown. Springer-Verlag.

Gardner, M. (1970), Mathematical games (The fantastic combinations of John Conway's new solitaire game "life"), *Scientific American* **223**, 20–123; also, (1971), On cellular automata, self-reproduction, the Garden of Eden and the game of "life," **224**, 112–117.

Gilmore, P. C. (1970), An examination of the geometry theorem machine, *Artificial Intelligence* **1**, 171–187.

Good, I. J. (1969), Analysis of the machine chess game, J. Scott (white), ICL-1900 versus R. D. Greenblatt, PDP-10, *Machine Intelligence* **4**, 267–269.

Greenblatt, R. D., D. E. Eastlake, and S. D. Crocker, (1967), *The Greenblatt chess program*, Tech. Report, Artificial Intelligence Project, MIT; [see Proceedings, AFIPS Fall Joint Computer Conference, 1967].

Levy, D. N. L. (1971), Computer chess—a case study on the CDC 6600, *Machine Intelligence* **6**, 151–163.

Scott, J. J. (1969), A chess-playing program, *Machine Intelligence* **4**, 255–265.

Selfridge, O. (1964), Reasoning in game playing by machines, *Computer Augmentation of Human Reasoning*, eds. Margo Sass and W. D. Wilkinson, Spartan Books.

Spencer, D. D. (1968), *Game Playing With Computers*, Spartan Books.

Stewart, I. (1971), The number of possible games of chess, *Journal of Recreational Mathematics* **4**, # 1, 50.

Wang, H. (1963), *A Survey of Mathematical Logic*. North-Holland; cf. Ch. IX, "Toward mechanical mathematics."

Waterman, D. A. (1970), Generalization learning techniques for automating the learning of heuristics, *Artificial Intelligence* **1**, 121–170.

9 Tricks Computers Play

Whenever we read that the election board's computer threw half the Democrat's votes to the Republican or that the electronic calculator down in the basement of First National Goldplate sent someone a check for $50 million instead of $50, we can never *really* be sure whether what went wrong was the computer itself or the man in the shadow—the programmer whose recipe happened to be cooking at the time the soufflé collapsed. There are at least three important ways for things to go awry. And which of these is/are involved usually can be determined only by access to both the computer and the program.

The worst thing that can go wrong is that the computer is actually sick. One of its transistors died, or one of its index registers is dropping a bit, or... Large computer installations usually have factory-trained mechanics present (actually they are usually called Customer Engineers) who are able to detect the cause of distress and supply a replacement which puts things aright again. And until International Bit Cruncher can put out a Model 9697 with long-lived transistors and overload-safe gates, the CE's are an indispensable part of the machine room crew.

A disconcerting aberration of computers that we occasionally encounter is one which makes the computer *appear* to look sick when actually the machine itself is perfect but there is a flaw in the operating system. (When a manufacturer sells his computer to a buyer, he usually sells—as part of a package—some master programs that go along with the machine; these master programs, along with the machine itself and its peripheral equipment, constitute the operating system.) A subtle error in the monitor programs or compilers (i.e., programs that translate from the user's program language into the machine's own language) has caused the trouble. Since the programming staff back at International Bit Cruncher are assumed to be ace programmers, IBC can usually be persuaded that *it* is responsible for the error only if it is confronted with well-documented evidence. But this kind of error is fortunately infrequent.

Now we come to a fundamental source of difficulty—one for which no one need be responsible—which must be coped with using all the cleverness that both the manufacturer and the user-programmer can muster. The difficulty stems from the *finiteness* of the computer. This finiteness is confronted both with respect to cell size and number of cells, but it is the cell size which preoccupies us at the moment.

To see how this finiteness poses an obstacle in the ordinary course of events, consider the problem of computing the Fibonacci sequence* on an actual machine—in this case the Control Data 6400. The cell size (or word size) of the CDC 6400 is 60 bits (binary digits), but since reading 60-bit words tends to strain human patience, when we command the computer to print out the actual content of cells, we do so asking for the octal rather than the binary version. In the present case, our arithmetic problem is to compute the sequence defined recursively by

$$F_0 = 0,$$
$$F_1 = 1,$$
$$F_{n+2} = F_{n+1} + F_n \qquad (n \geq 0).$$

Suppose that we want the first hundred numbers in this sequence, and that we ask the computer to print these out, starting with F_2. We might expect the following FORTRAN program to do the trick:

---

* This sequence is ubiquitous in mathematics. It appeared first in an arithmetic text *Liber Abbaci* (Book of the Abacus), written by Leonardo Pisano (*alias* Leonardo Fibonacci) in 1202. The sequence arises in the calculation of the number of rabbits which have accumulated in a year, breeding according to Fibonacci's rules. A miniature treatise on the sequence may be found in Martin Gardner, Mathematical games: the multiple fascinations of the Fibonacci sequence, *Scientific American* **220** (March, 1969), 116–119.

```
      L = 0
      K = 1
      DO 5 I = 2, 100
      M = K + L
      PRINT 6, I, M, M
      L = K
    5 K = M
    6 FORMAT (I6, I25, O25)
      STOP
```

(At each stage of iteration, we are saving the current values of F_n, F_{n+1}, and F_{n+2} in the cells designated L, K, and M respectively; the only care we must take in the program is to be sure to move the value in cell K to cell L before moving the value from cell M to cell K.) According to the program, the PRINT command is going to produce the value of the current F_n twice—its decimal version *and* its octal version—in each line of output. Why ask for the same thing twice? The answer is that the octal version is precisely the content of the cell, whereas the decimal version is an artifact produced by some conversion routine that belongs to the operating system; and while we may have confidence in the ability of the conversion routine to correctly compute the decimal version from the octal (really binary) version, nevertheless it is comforting to have the actual pre-conversion number available at times . . . like this one.

So the computer races through this computation. The beginning of the print-out goes:

2	1	000000000000000000001
3	2	000000000000000000002
4	3	000000000000000000003
5	5	000000000000000000005
6	8	000000000000000000010
7	13	000000000000000000015
⋮	⋮	⋮

And everything looks fine ... until we arrive at the computation of the F_{71} when the output takes on a curious appearance:

$\vdots$	$\vdots$	$\vdots$
68	72723460248141	00002042210000751115
69	117669030460994	00003260236460577102
70	190392490709135	00005322446461550217
71	R	00010602705142347321
72	R	00016125353624117540
73	R	00026730260766467061
74	R	00045055634612606621
75	R	00074006115601275702
76	R	00141063752414104523
77	R	00235072070215402425
78	R	00376156042631507150
79	R	00633250133047111575
80	R	01231426175700620745
81	R	02064676330747732542
82	R	03316324526650553507
83	R	05403223057620506251
84	R	10721547606471261760
85	R	16324772666311770231
86	R	27246542475003252211
87	R	45573535363315242442
88	R	75042300060320514653
89	R	42636035443635757316
$\vdots$	$\vdots$	$\vdots$

There are two points of interest here; one is incidental but the other is fundamental. First, the appearance of the letter R in place of the expected number is merely a peculiar idiosyncrasy of the input/output routine (which is part of the CDC operating system) which has the responsibility of providing a decimal image of the binary number which the program is to output. This particular output routine prevents us from obtaining (directly) the values of F_n ($n \geq 71$), although the computer has correctly calculated (at least several of) these values; in fact, we can check the correctness by simply adding the octal representations, in octal of course, and checking that the numbers in the rightmost column are correctly generated ... as they are until we get to F_{89}.

Here we come to the fundamental difficulty. The addition of F_{88} to F_{87} produces a number which is just too big to fit into a 60-bit cell. The addition should be as follows:

```
 45573535363315242442
 75042300060320514653
 ────────────────────
142636035443635757315
```

But if we look at F_{89}, we see that we have lost the leading digit (usually refered to as *overflow*) and moreover the last digit, which we expect to be 5 is presented as 6. This latter apparent anomaly gives an incorrect last digit but nevertheless actually reflects the strategy of computer designers, who, for this machine, have chosen to use *one's complement arithmetic* for addition*. The difficulty here is simply due to the overflow, and once overflow occurs, as in the present case, any further computation may be quite meaningless.

If overflow can seriously impair a computation, do computers accordingly signal some warning when overflow occurs? Surprisingly enough, some computers do and some do not. The CDC 6400, in the above case, does not. But consider, then, some interesting consequences of this failure to provide a warning. Suppose that a programmer wished to compute F_{93} as an octal number and was uninterested in the preceding values (F_n, $n \leq 92$); he might very well merely compute as above, but print-out only the value of F_{93}. In the above case there would be no

---

* In one's complement arithmetic a number with leading bit equal to zero is considered positive, a number with leading bit equal to one is considered negative, and the negative of any number is obtained by taking its one's complement, i.e., replacing zeros by ones and ones by zeros. In the addition of such numbers, the overflow bit is added into the result at the low-order end of the number (hence the 6 in F_{89}).

indication that the value which appears is incorrect. (But the nonzero leading digit of the result might raise a suspicion as to whether overflow *had* occurred; on the other hand, F_{94} is here proffered as 0763 . . . . and a naive programmer might look at that and say: lucky we wanted only F_{94}, if we'd gone higher, we might have overflowed.)

As we saw above, 15-digit integers are about the largest that we can get in the course of computation with the CDC 6400.* But many scientific calculations involve very large numbers and/or very small numbers and perhaps not very many significant digits. So most computers have an alternate way of dealing with numbers: the *floating-point* representation. This representation splits up the cell, in a sense, and (for the CDC 6400) uses one part (the first bit) to hold the sign, just as before, and one part (bits 2, 3, . . , 12) to hold an exponent e, and the remaining 48 bits to hold a coefficient C. The number being represented is then $\pm C \cdot 2^e$, except for one little detail: The exponent e is actually the intended exponent with 2000 (octal) added on. (This is called *biasing* the exponent.)

Of course, using the floating-point mode means that there are 11 less significant bits to work with, but the enormous range of values which are available makes the loss less painful. (The range is about $10^{-294} \leq |x| \leq 10^{322}$, and zero, of course.)

We can repeat the calculation of the Fibonacci sequence, but now using floating-point values rather than integer (or *fixed-point*) values. If we do, and again ask for the octal version of the numbers calculated as values of the F_n as well as the decimal versions, we get the following result:

n	F_n	F_n
2	.10000000000000E + 01	1720400000000000000
3	.20000000000000E + 01	1721400000000000000
4	.30000000000000E + 01	1721600000000000000

---

* "Largest" here means with respect to the repertoire of normal machine instructions. One can always write programs which permit arithmetic with very large integers—chopping up such integers and keeping the parts in separate cells—but the corresponding computation of arithmetic tends to be relatively slow.

5	.50000000000000E + 01	17225000000000000000
6	.80000000000000E + 01	17234000000000000000
7	.13000000000000E + 02	17236400000000000000
.	.	.
.	.	.
.	.	.

In the decimal version of F_n the trailing E + 01 stands for 10^1, and E + 02 stands for 10^2 (interpreted as a factor multiplying the number to its left). In the octal version of F_n, the first four octal digits (e.g., 1720) form the exponent, and the remaining sixteen octal digits form the coefficient (e.g., 4000000000000000). The coefficients look rather large, but this is simply because the corresponding 48-bit binary number is required to have a leading 1; but although the coefficient here (say for F_2) is 4000000000000000 = 2^{47}, the floating-point representation compensates for this by subtracting 47 from the biased exponent. Note that since F_3 is $2 \cdot F_2$, the exponent of (the floating-point representation of) F_3 is larger by one than the exponent of F_2.

The computation of F_n in floating-point gets safely past the stage where the integer computation ran into trouble, i.e., at F_{71} (actually, remember, it was not the computation itself but rather the conversion that went awry at F_{71}):

70	.19039249070913E + 15	20005322446461550217
71	.30806152117013E + 15	20014301342461163550
72	.49845401187926E + 15	20017052565712047656
73	.80651553304939E + 15	20025566054175515613
74	.13049695449286E + 16	20034505563461260661
.	.	.
.	.	.
.	.	.
.	.	.
99	.21892299583455E + 21	20245736125343166247
100	.35422484817925E + 21	20254631733355237045

In the integer computation of F_n the computer got as far as F_{88} = 75042300060320514653 (octal), before going awry. The coefficient in the floating-point computation of F_{88} is the last 16 digits of 20147504230006032043. Comparison of the two representations shows that only 14 significant digits are correct in the floating-point re-presentation (whereas all of the 20 digits of the integer computation are correct). What is happening in the case of the floating-point computation is that the more significant figures, and the order of magnitude, tend to remain correct, while error builds up the low-order digits. This error is generated because as the length of the values of the F_n increases, there comes a point when significant figures are lost at the low-order end of the cell. And thereafter, of course, the values are incorrect—but usually still leaving enough correct high-order significant figures so that the answer is meaningful.

Clearly in very long calculations which use floating-point arithmetic the danger of serious error of this type (usually refered to as *rounding error*) is important. If the results of such calculations are to be believed, there must be some associated mathematical analysis that gives a bound on how large the error might be, or at least some type of empirical evidence that the results are actually trustworthy. In the absence of either such analysis or evidence, computation tends to lose something of its scientific character and begins to slip into numerology.

A surprisingly tricky aspect of computing with finite computers is that the same sort of confounding developments (as suggested above) can occur easily without long sequences of operations necessarily being in-volved. It is easy to pose quite simple and brief computational problems in such a way that the (computational) confrontation with the finiteness of computer word size is immediate. In an amusing but cautionary essay*, G. E. Forsythe has presented a collection of just such examples. We consider several of these:

Suppose that the following computation is to be performed on a decimal machine that has an unusually modest word size; its floating-point hard-ware allows just three significant digits. On this machine a program is used to compute the solution to the pair of simultaneous linear equations,

$$0.000100\ x + 1.00y = 1.00,$$
$$1.00\ x + 1.00y = 2.00.$$

---

* G. E. Forsythe, Pitfalls in computation, or why a math book isn't enough, *TR CS 147*, Stanford University, 1970.

If the program performs the Gaussian elimination algorithm, the first step is to multiply the first equation by 10,000 and the second step is to subtract this multiplied equation from the second equation. This eliminates the variable x. The first step produces

$$9999 \, y = 9998,$$

which, rounded to the three significant digits of our current machine, yields

$$10,000 \, y = 10,000.$$

The back solution, from the three-digit machine, is

$$y = 1.00,$$
$$x = 0.00. \tag{*}$$

But since the exact solution to the original pair of equations is $x = 10,000/9999$, $y = 9998/9999$, we see that rounding the exact solution to three significant digits yields

$$x = 1.00,$$
$$y = 1.00. \tag{**}$$

The divergence between (*) and (**) is startling. It can be traced to the fact that a critical part of the arithmetic is lost under the rounding to three significant figures, and this, in turn, can be traced to the fact that the leading coefficient in the first of the original equations is very small, compared to the other coefficients. This suggests that Gaussian elimination should be modified so that the largest pertinent coefficients are used first. Thus if the original equations are first interchanged and *then* Gaussion elimination is used, the result from three-digit machine is $x = 1.00$, $y = 1.00$ (a triumph!).

One disconcerting aspect of the previous example is the fact that two different algorithmic procedures (i.e., programs) may be mathematically equivalent, yet—on a finite-word-length machine—produce different solutions to the same problem. Of course, in the preceding example various calculated solutions can be substituted into the equations and the apparent exactness of the solutions can be compared. This would immediately void the candidate $y = 1.00$, $x = 0.00$. But now another disconcerting aspect presents itself in the form of an example due to C. B. Moler:

For the pair of simultaneous equations

$$0.780\,x + 0.563\,y - 0.217 = 0,$$
$$0.913\,x + 0.659\,y - 0.254 = 0,$$

two alternative solutions are proposed:

$$(x_1, y_1) = (0.999, -1.001)$$

and

$$(x_2+, y_2) = (0.341, -0.087).$$

Which is better? Substituting these candidate solutions into the equations yields:

$$0.780\,x_1 + 0.563\,y_1 - 0.217 = -0.001243$$
$$0.913\,x_1 + 0.569\,y_1 - 0.254 = -0.001572$$

and

$$0.780\,x_2 + 0.563\,y_2 - 0.217 = -0.000001$$
$$0.913\,x_2 + 0.569\,y_2 - 0.254 = 0$$

so one might tend to accept (x_2, y_2) as the better solution. Yet the correct solution is $(x, y) = (1, -1)$. The immediate moral is that a problem should be well posed with respect to whatever criterion decides the acceptability of a proposed solution; one might go further and suggest that the instinctive approach may lead to numerology, while the subtle approach leads to numerical analysis.

REFERENCES

Forsythe, G. E. (1970), Pitfalls in computation, or why a math book isn't enough, *Tech. Rep. CS 147*. Stanford University.

Householder, A. S. (1964) *The Theory of Matrices in Numerical Analysis*. Blaisdell.

Knuth, D. E. (1969), Seminumerical algorithms. *The Art of Computer Programming*, Vol. 2. Addison-Wesley.

Ralston, A. (1965) *A First Course in Numerical Analysis*. McGraw-Hill.

Wilkinson, J. H. (1963) *Rounding Errors in Algebraic Processes*. Prentice-Hall.

10 Artificial Intelligence and Intelligent Artifice

"Echo IV," wrote Echo IV, far away in the calm remoteness of the Rothermere Vulgarian Ethics Wing, "is a brilliant new arrival on the literary scene. *The Tin Men* is its first novel, and critics who have seen it prior to publication . . ."*

Michael Frayn

. . . .

Studies of artificial intelligence (or "machine intelligence," as it is sometimes called) have the dual objective of trying to obtain machines which, in problematical situations, would respond as intelligent humans would, and trying to obtain an understanding of what human intelligence is, by a thorough understanding of artificial intelligence.

A great deal of effort in these studies has gone into creating capable game-playing programs and robot-control programs. In the latter applications the computer acts as a brain which dictates to servo-mechanisms which control prosthetic devices (or perhaps carts), acting upon its interpretation of visual information fed to the computer by a video camera. The program must process the optical data which it receives and

---

* Michael Frayn, *The Tin Men*. Little, Brown. 1965. Copyright © 1965 by Michael Frayn. Reprinted by permission.

identify images and assess angles and distances; it must then compute to what degree it must rotate wheels, extend arms, manipulate fingers, and then send the corresponding signals to the control devices and servo-mechanisms.

Unfortunately the robot action, so far obtained, seems to accord with a rather stunted intelligence. A short but brilliantly produced film (*Butterfinger*, Stanford University Artificial Intelligence Project) features a robot arm trying to fulfill the goal of gathering together into a single pile a small scattered collection of children's building blocks. The stacking of the blocks is performed in a pathetically slow and clumsy way, suggesting the Herculean computing task involved in processing the optical data provided by the video camera.

The speed with which living creatures cope with considerably more complicated situations seems to be due to the ability of the animal brain to process an enormous amount of information in parallel—as if the brain consisted of a large number of computers, each processing its part of the data at the same time—whereas the digital computer must process all of the data sequentially, one step at a time*. Of course, there is a much faster signal generation and propagation in the digital computer, so that the parallel processing ability of the brain (which, for the individual elements, is very slow in comparison with the digital computer) loses out to the computer in certain types of information processing.

The question is sometimes raised as to what delineates artificial intelligence programs from *any* kind of program which performs an analysis that a human mind would otherwise be called upon to do. Is there any real difference between an algorithm which tries to find a solution to a set of logical equations and an algorithm which tries to find a mate-in-

---

* ILLIAC IV, mentioned earlier, seems to represent the latest advance into designing parallel capability into digital computers; and its degree of parallelism, in comparison with that of the brain, is meager indeed. The *theory* of parallel computation is in its initial stage of development; cf. R. M. Karp and R. E. Miller (1969), Parallel program schemata, *Journal of Computer and System Sciences* **3**, 147–195.

two? In principle the answer, of course, is "no." And this holds true even where the computer is delivering output in an area where the meaning of algorithmics is often much less clearcut—the computer-creation of artistic and aesthetic constructions.

The use of computers as creative instruments in the fields of music and painting are well known. But in the field of literary creativity, notable developments have been surprisingly sparse. Outside of the Echo IV program (which is acknowledged to be unique and likely to remain so, for some time) we know of only one other such program—Pourboireki's* algorithm in the closely related field of computational poetics (the *Reverse V* program†).

Pourboireki developed his early versions (Reverses I and II) of the program at the University of California, Berkeley, early in the 1960s. The program takes as input any short subject-phrase and an indication as to whether the output is to be brief or extended. The program then outputs some rhymes which presumably satisfy the input conditions.

Pourboireki, a generally acknowledged eccentric, formally works only one day a year, usually April 1 (which he says is the only symbolically appropriate day for any type of labor). On 1 April 1966 he exhibited, at the Berkeley Computer Center, the first output from the debugged Reverse I. He drew very little response from the Center (which was largely peopled with humanists, in those days) and none whatever from the English Department (which is not surprising, in view of its well-known attitude toward mechanical production and its traditional inclination to ignore anything written later than the eighteenth century). Pourboireki's reaction to this rebuff was reflected perhaps in his titling of the computer output ("A Big Stout Naught"). The output had the appearance:

---

* Nicolas Pourboireki is the great grandson of the obscure Ukrainian general and mathematician Nicolai Ivanovich Pourboireki.

† Pourboireki originally named the program *REV-UP* (for Recursive Enumeration of Verse Universing Program).

```
BIT  BY  BIT
WORD  BY  WORD
FIT  BY  FIT
TENDING  TOWARD

BYTE  BY  BYTE
LINE  BY  LINE
LEFT  TO  RIGHT
VERSE  DESIGN

LINE  BY  LINE
COUPLED  TIGHT
TIGER,  TIGER
BURNING  BRIGHT
```

(Several members of the University's Institute for Human Development, after mulling over the output from Reverse I, suggested the creation of a parallel Institute for Machine Development—a notion which attracted the support of several engineering departments—but the University had recently bought several Nobelists and was disinclined toward new ventures.)

Pourboireki disappeared, as was his wont, and nothing more might have been heard of the computational poetics project, had the following letter not been received at the Computer Center:

4th May 1967

To: The Director
    Computer Center
    University of California at Berkeley
    California, USA

Dear Sir:

I wonder if I could make an enquiry of you that borders dangerously on facetiousness.

We are interested in doing a feature in our magazine on computer poetry—poetry actually composed by computers—and the University of California has been suggested to me as possibly dabbling in this sphere as part of its research.

We would like to get some information on this aspect of computers and, if possible, to get some poetry written for us in this way.

It is, I'm afraid, a somewhat monstrous request to make of you, but if you do anything along these lines or have some information as to who does, I would be most grateful for your assistance.

Yours sincerely,

. . . . . .

Features Editor
The Condé Nast Publications Ltd. Vogue House, Hanover Square,
London WI. Grosvenor 9080

The usual course of events when requests of unusual character, such as this, arrive is that they are dispatched to the appropriate expert, who is then left with the responsibility for satisfying them. In the present case this posed an obstacle: Only Pourboireki had been working in computational poetics and he would not be putting in his working day for another eleven months. Nevertheless, the Vogue letter was shown to him and he was invited to reply.

Pourboireki's reaction, upon reading the letter, was one of amused skepticism. The letter, he said, was obviously facetious—its first line was meant to make that clear—or else it was a fraud: No one could seriously expect polite response from a computational poetics project after referring to its work as "dabbling in this sphere." Nor would Pourboireki respond to entreaties to accept the letter as in good faith—until it was discovered that, according to the Center's accounting records, Pourboireki had not actually worked on the preceding April 1 but had been paid as if he did!

Reverse II was at once brought out of the program files and Pourboireki punched a few data cards. The only question was: How many poems should the computer run off? One thousand, one hundred, or just a dozen or so? The initial suggestion was that fifty be run off and the best dozen of these be sent on to London. But Pourboireki demurred. Run a dozen, he said, and whatever comes out, comes out; it's not a silly poetry contest—it's just a demonstration.

So within an hour or so, the computer output was in the mail to England, along with a covering letter:

Features Editor
VOGUE
Condé Nast Publications Ltd
Vogue House
Hanover Square, London W1, England

Dear . . . . . . :

Your letter concerning computer-produced poetry has found its way into my hands. We of course expect a certain irrepressible element of facetiousness from features editors, but experience has shown that unyielding patience and determined tact may often result in correspondence of entertainment value, if not serious interest, to both sides.

Turning to your specific inquiry, if by "poetry" you mean "rhymes," then the answer to your question is *yes*, the computer produces poetry. If by "poetry" you mean poetry, then you must be informed that there has been serious difficulty in dealing with the computer in this particular domain. (In the latter case, as you may surmise, the trouble stems primarily from our inability to determine precisely when the computer is in a creative mood: If we insist upon mechanical production of lyrically fragile material, finely polished and hauntingly evocative, we find that the response from the computer is usually sullen silence or—on rare but embarrassing occasion—obscene vulgarisms, tersely rhymed.)

In all fairness to the computer, it must be remembered that the computer intrinsically produces nothing whatever: It is actually a program within the computer which effects what is required as, in fact, compelled by some person who constructed the program itself. . . .

Hoping that this may be of some value to you,

Your obedient servant,

Nicholas Pourboireki
Computational poetics

Pourboireki gave, in his letter, a sketchy and not particularly revealing account of how the program Reverse II worked. (He would perhaps have done better by simply pointing out that the principle of operation of Reverse II was identical to that of Echo IV.)

Part of the computer output that accompanied the letter had the following appearance:

```
SUBJECT = ANSWER TO VOGUE QUERY RE COMP POETICS
QUALITY = ARBITRARY
```

              I, SILENT MACHINE,
              ALERT TO YOUR ORDER,
              ANSWER YOUR QUERY,
              DANGEROUS BORDER,

              SILENT MACHINING,
              VERSE-ED REDUCTION,
              NO INTERVENING,
              POETIC CONSTRUCTION,

              SILENT MECHANICS,
              METERED ALONG LINES,
              ALGORITHMICALLY PANICS,
              PRODUCES THE WRONG LINES

```
SUBJECT = REFLEXIVE POETICS
QUALITY = ARBITRARY
```

              TO RECUR ENDLESSLY,
              TO SENSE THE GENERATIONS REELING
              INTO EXISTENCE
              IN IDENTICAL MILLIONS
              OF WHICH EACH
              IS A PAINED UNWILLING COPY OF WHAT
              CAME BEFORE

```
SUBJECT = POETS VS MACHINES
QUALITY = ARBITRARY
```

              POETS DISLIKE COMPUTING POETICS,
              MECHANICAL MINDED DISPLEASES AESTHETICS,
              POETS SPLIT ART WITH THE SOUL'S MUDDY
              PRISM,
              MACHINES SPLIT APART,
              STUDY THE SCHISM

```
SUBJECT = POETICA AMERICANA
QUALITY = SUCCINCT
```

              ALL GOD'S CHILLUN GOT ALGORITHM

When, about a year later, Pourboireki turned up on April 1, he was asked, along with more important requests, to run the current version (Reverse III) on the subject of "computer science"—a phrase in which the University was beginning to entertain a superficial interest. Unfortunately Pourboireki was unaware of the latest system changes and fed the program to the computer with too large a time limit . . . one minute. This resulted in the computation of a fifty pound bale of rhymes, the content of which has remained largely unknown—no one has read past the first 1000 pages or so, of output. The output begins:

```
SUBJECT  =  COMPUTER SCIENCE
QUALITY  =  EXTENDED
                AT THE OUTSET,
                NOTICE BABBAGE,
                AND HIS PLAN FOR CALCULATORS,
                AND HIS FRIEND THE SUCCINCT SIREN,
                DAUGHTER OF THE POET BYRON
                WHOSE QUICK BRILLIANCE BRISKLY RANGING
                STATED THAT A PROGRAM CHANGING

                COULD IN FACT BE DONE BETWEEN
                THE PROGRAM AND THE QUICK MACHINE,
                EMPHASIZING THIS WOULD MEAN
                NO HUMAN HAND WOULD INTERVENE,
                LADY LOVELACE THUS ENSURING
                ABSTRACT NOTIONS NAMED FOR TURING

                     .

                     .

                     .
```

One student, after reading part of the output, suggested rerunning the program—constraining the computation to blank verse—and using the expected output as scripts for several courses in the subject. The suggestion, while undeservedly cynical, was provocative enough to lead some of the staff to request that the University provide machine time for the rerun. Unfortunately the state government had further tightened the screws of its financial economies program, leaving the University unable to muster financial support for another minute of running time. Those members of the faculty who felt that they could benefit from the project contributed donations to fund the computation, but by the time that formal arrangements had been secured, Pourboireki had departed for another year.

The evolution of the program (Reverses V and VI) has levelled off in capability in a way which—in Pourboireki's view—has some disturbing implications for artificial intelligence. His point is made by the output generated to serve as lyrics for a song ("Sky divers' Lament" for the film *The Gypsy Moths*):

SUBJECT = SKY DIVERS LAMENT / THE GYPSY MOTHS

QUALITY = ROGERS AND HART

> FALLING IN LOVE WITH FALLING
> IS FALLING FOR SOMETHING NEW,
> FALLING IN LOVE WITH FALLING
> IS SOMETHING OUT OF THE BLUE
>
> FALLING IN LOVE WITH FALLING
> HAS SIMPLY BREATHTAKING PACE,
> FALLING IN LOVE WITH FALLING
> REQUIRES A LOT OF SPACE
>
> I FELL IN LOVE WITH FALLING
> ONE NIGHT WHEN THE MOON WAS NEW,
> FALLING IS GROOVY
> AT LEAST IN A MOVIE,
> AND WHAT A VIEW
>
> I TOOK TO FLIGHT
> AS A MOTH SEEKS THE LIGHT
> IN A SOMBER WORLD,
> BUT I FAILED TO WEIGH,
> ONE OMINOUS DAY,
> HOW MY CHUTE WAS CURLED
>
> I FELL OUT OF LOVE WITH FALLING
> ONE NIGHT WHEN THE MOON WAS WANE,
> AT FIVE THOUSAND FEET

```
I SLIPPED INTO SLEET
AND A DRIVING RAIN
FALLING,S APPALLING,
IT,S SIMPLY A STALLING
IN EMPTY SPACE,
FALLING TOO FAR
CAN END IN A JAR
IF YOU LAND OFF BASE
FALLING IN LOVE WITH FALLING
IS JEOPARDY, SOMETHING TO JEER,
FALLING IN LOVE WITH FALLING
IS QUEER IN THE INNER EAR
******** LINE LIMIT EXCEEDED ******
```

Hollywood has so far rejected this, and other, lyrics from Reverse VI, claiming that the output is "dated," "square," and that the work of current lyricists under contract is "already too mechanical according to industry standards." The problem, then, according to Pourboireki, is not to construct artificial intelligence programs that effectively mimic human creativity, but rather programs that mimic *talented* human creativity.* In this respect, Reverse VI may be typical of the work to come —barely creative and unyieldingly talentless—and Echo IV may be that rare, happy accident that is unlikely to occur readily again.

REFERENCES

Collens, R. J. (1970), Computer generated poetry as a pedagogical tool, *Proceedings of a Conference on Interdisciplinary Research in Computer*

---

* A. M. Turing anticipated this very problem in his *Can Machines Think?* [Cf. *World of Mathematics*, ed. J. R. Newman. Simon & Shuster, 1956 (Vol. IV)], offering the conjectural human/computer conversation:

Q: Please write me a sonnet on the subject of the Forth Bridge.
A: Count me out on this one. I could never write poetry.

Science, M. G. Saunders and R. G. Stanton, eds. Winnipeg: University of Manitoba.

Leed, J. (1966), *The Computer & Literary Style: Introductory Essays and Studies*. Kent State University Press.

Lincoln, Harry B. (1970), *The Computer and Music*. Cornell University Press.

Lincoln, Harry B. (1970), The current state of music research and the computer, *Computers and the Humanities* 5.

Milic, Louis T. "The Possible Usefulness of Poetry Generation," *Proceedings of the Symposium on Literary and Linguistic Uses of the Computer* (Cambridge University, March 24–26, 1970), ed. Roy A. Wisbey, Cambridge University Press. [Cited in *Computers and the Humanities* 5, No. 2 (1970).]

Part II   A View from Without: the digital villain

Prologue

"In from three to eight years we will have a machine with the general intelligence of an average human being. I mean a machine that will be able to read Shakespeare, grease a car, play office politics, tell a joke, have a fight. At that point the machine will begin to educate itself with fantastic speed. In a few months it will be at genius level and a few months after that its powers will be incalculable."*

> Marvin Minsky,
> quoted by Brad Darrach,
> *Life Magazine*, November 20, 1970

"I hope that man and these ultimate machines will be able to collaborate without conflict. But if they can't, we may be forced to choose sides. And if it comes to a choice, I know what mine will be . . . My loyalties go to intelligent life, no matter in what medium it may arise."

> A computer-memory expert,
> quoted by Darrach, *ibid*

Dr. Marvin Minsky, professor of electrical engineering of the Massachusetts Institute of Technology and a pioneer in the field of artificial intelligence, says that "our pious skeptics told us that machines would never sense things. Now that the machines can see complex shapes, our skeptics tell us that

---

* From "Meet Shaky, the First Electronic Person," by Brad Darrach, *Life* Magazine, November 20, 1970, © 1970 Time Inc.

they can never know that they sense things." But, he advises, "do not be bullied by authoritative pronouncements about what machines will never do. Such statements are based on pride, not fact. There has emerged no hint, in any scientific theory of machines, of limitations not shared by man. The rate of evolution of machines is millions of times faster, because we can combine separate improvements directly, where nature depends upon fortuitous events of recombination."*

> David Rorvik,
> "Slaves or Masters?"
> *Playboy Magazine*, July, 1969

. . . .

Computers can be programmed to "think" in much the same sense that they can be programmed to produce "random" numbers. In both cases, suitable tests are agreed upon, and if the computer response satisfies the tests, then its behavior can be said to satisfy the characteristics which the tests define. Of course some people say that all this is just a Humpty-Dumpty facade: Computer-produced numbers are not really random, and computer-produced chess play is not really thinking. (For, there are *some* tests that these numbers should, but do not, satisfy; and there are *some* intelligence tests that artificial intelligence does not satisfy.) But this is somewhat beside the point. There are, and will be, artificially intelligent machines, and they will have to be contended with, just as members of society contend with each other—with relationships constantly shifting and evolving.

One aspect of artificial intelligence evolution that is particularly compelling is the speed of its development. In part, this speed derives from a refinement in technology: As faster, more efficient computers are designed, the artificial intelligence programs which they effect become concomitantly more powerful. There seems, moreover, to be a kind of Parkinson's law which governs the obsession of the establishment with the refinement of technology. Most of the viewpoints which we consider in Part II exhibit a common theme of anxiety that stems from this refinement.

---

* Reprinted by permission of *Playboy* Magazine.

Reading history is a scary enterprise. Post-history (sometimes called "science fiction"), with its deliciously unlikely little terrorisms, used to be enjoyably diverting; but lately it has been blending persistently into reality and we suddenly find that, when the story becomes too harsh, we cannot end it simply by closing the book.

11 *R.U.R. (Rossum's Universal Robots):* man as machine

Robert Bolt said (in his Preface to *A Man for All Seasons*) that Society "can only have as much idea as we have what we are about, for it has only our brains to think with."

But that was Yesterday.

The day before yesterday—about 1920—Karel Capek wrote a remarkable play entitled *R.U.R. (Rossum's Universal Robots).** The Robots are the product of a thriving commercial enterprise which, sensitive even in that day to the danger of industrial espionage, is located on a remote island. There a handful of men—scientists and engineers, all straight types—go about their humdrum tasks of building up production and assessing the market. The factory which they control produces a cunning facsimile of a human (the classical model for a robot). The Robots are turned out in both male and female form, are genuinely humanlike in appearance and speech, and are rather surprisingly inexpensive. (As the play opens, the General Manager is acknowledging an order from a New York firm for five thousand Robots.)

Faithful to formula, Capek gets the boy-meets-girl development underway at once with the arrival, on the island, of a beautiful young woman,

---

* Excerpts of the play *R.U.R. (Rossum's Universal Robots)* appearing in this chapter are reprinted by permission of Samuel French, Inc. Copyright, 1923 by Doubleday, Page and Company.

Helena Glory, daughter of Professor William Glory, of St. Trydeswyde's, Oxbridge (or was it Camford?) Helena is—surely even by the standards of the nineteen twenties—*square*. And, as is regrettably often the case with beautiful girls, Helena is somewhat obtuse. (So much for the daughters of English dons at Oxbridge.)

Visitors to the island are evidently frequent and Domain—the General Manager—seems to be bored with their relentless uniformity:

Helena. I have come here——

Domain. To have a look at our factory where people are made. Like all visitors. Well, there's no objection.

Helena. I thought it was forbidden——

Domain. It is forbidden to enter the factory, of course. But everybody comes here with an introduction and then——

Helena. And you show everybody——?

Domain. Only certain things. The manufacture of artificial people is a secret process.

Helena. If you only knew how enormously that——

Domain. Interests me, you were going to say. Europe's talking about nothing else.

Helena. Why don't you let me finish speaking?

Domain. I beg your pardon. Did you want to say anything else?

Helena. I only wanted to ask——

Domain. Whether I could make a special exception in your case and show you our factory. Certainly, Miss Glory.

Helena. How do you know that I wanted to ask you that?

Domain. They all do. [*standing up.*] We shall consider it a special honor to show you more than the rest, because—indeed—I mean——

Helena. Thank you.

Domain. But you must undertake not to divulge the least——

Helena [*standing up and giving him her hand*]. My word of honor.

Domain. Thank you. Won't you raise your veil?

The invitation is answered to the General Manager's satisfaction. He then gives a brief resume of how the old physiologist Rossum and his nephew—the young engineer Rossum—developed the Robot. This involves a bit of technology concerning their internal construction as well, none of it clarifying the picture at all. But there is nothing obscure about the motivation for production. The General Manager asks his young visitor what she thinks the best type of worker is:

> *Helena.* The best? Perhaps the one who is most honest and hard-working.
>
> *Domain.* No, the cheapest. The one whose needs are the smallest. Young Rossum invented a worker with the minimum of requirements. He had to simplify him. He rejected everything that did not contribute directly to the progress of work. In this way he rejected everything that makes man more expensive. In fact, he rejected man and made the Robot. My dear Miss Glory, the Robots are not people. Mechanically they are more perfect than we are, they have an enormously developed intelligence, but they have no soul. Have you ever seen what a Robot looks like inside?
>
> *Helena.* Good gracious, no!
>
> *Domain.* Very neat, very simple. Really a beautiful piece of work. Not much in it, but everything in flawless order. The product of an engineer is technically at a higher pitch of perfection than a product of nature.

The currently produced Robots come in a variety of grades. Of course, they have a built-in obsolescence factor—the best wear out in about twenty years. But the quality of the best seems to be rather good. Domain introduces his secretary to Helena—the secretary is a surprisingly knowledgeable young female who speaks four languages—and states that the secretary is a Robot. Helena says, what nonsense, she is not going to be taken in by some silly advertising stunt. But in fact the secretary, Sulla, *is* a Robot and a credit to the assembly line. Helena is unconvinced. Verifying that a perfect facsimile of a human is *not* a human is a tricky problem, and Domain's solution is to indicate his readiness to prove his claim by sending Sulla to the stamping mill! Another Robot, Marius, comes onto the scene and is ordered to escort Sulla to oblivion. And how does Sulla react to all this?

> *Helena* [*embracing Sulla*]. Don't be afraid, Sulla, I won't let you go. Tell me, darling, are they always so cruel to you? You mustn't put up with that, Sulla. You mustn't.

Sulla. I am a Robot.

Helena. That doesn't matter. Robots are just as good as we are. Sulla, you wouldn't let yourself be cut to pieces.

Sulla. Yes.

Helena. Oh, you're not afraid of death, then?

Sulla. I cannot tell, Miss Glory.

Helena. Do you know what would happen to you there?

Sulla. Yes, I should cease to move.

Helena. How dreadful.

Domain. Marius, tell Miss Glory what you are.

Marius. Marius, the Robot.

Domain. Would you take Sulla into the testing room?

Marius. Yes.

Domain. Would you be sorry for her?

Marius. I cannot tell.

Domain. What would happen to her?

Marius. She would cease to move. They would put her into the stamping mill.

Domain. That is death, Marius. Aren't you afraid of death?

Marius. No.

Domain. You see, Miss Glory, the Robots are not attached to life. They have no reason to be. They have no enjoyments. They are less than so much grass.

Helena finds this dialogue convincing, and the Robots are dismissed. A few moments later the handful of (human) engineers and scientists who staff the island enter on their coffee break. Human females are a rarity on the island and only anachronism prevents their singing *There is nothing like a dame!* in the wings. Encountering Helena, they are uniformly delighted. She, in turn, is about to bestow upon them a frightful humiliation: She takes them to be Robots. Their deluge of questions is interrupted by Domain:

Domain. Be quiet, let Miss Glory speak.

Helena [*to Domain*].   What am I to speak to them about?

Domain [*surprised*]. About what you like.

Helena.   Shall . . . may I speak quite frankly?

Domain.   Why, of course.

Helena [*wavering, then with desperate resolution*]. Tell me, doesn't it ever distress you to be treated like this?

Fabry.   Treated?—Who by?

Helena.   Everybody.
[*All look at each other in consternation.*]

Alquist.   Treated?

Dr. Gall.   What makes you think that?

Helman.   Treated?

Berman.   Really!

Helena.   Don't you feel that you might be living a better life?

Dr. Gall.   Well, that depends what you mean, Miss Glory.

Helena.   I mean that—[*bursting out*] that it's perfectly outrageous. It's terrible. [*standing up.*] The whole of Europe is talking about how you're being treated. That's why I came here to see, and it's a thousand times worse than could have been imagined. How can you put up with it?

Alquist.   Put up with what?

Helena.   Your position here. Good heavens, you are living creatures just like us, like the whole of Europe, like the whole world. It's scandalous, disgraceful!

Berman.   Good gracious, Miss Glory.

Fabry.   Well boys, she's not so far out. We live here just like Red Indians.

Helena.   Worse than Red Indians. May, oh, may I call you brothers?

Berman.   Of course you may, why not?

Helena.   Brothers, I have not come here as my father's daughter. I have come on behalf of the Humanity League. Brothers, the Humanity League now has over two hundred thousand members. Two hundred thousand people are on your side and offer you their help.

Berman.   Two hundred thousand people, that's quite a tidy lot, Miss Glory, quite good.

Fabry.   I'm always telling you there's nothing like good old Europe. You see, they've not forgotten us. They're offering us help.

Dr. Gall. What help? A theatre?

Helman. An orchestra?

Helena. More than that.

Alquist. Just you?

Helena. Oh, never mind about me. I'll stay as long as is necessary.

Berman. By Jove, that's good.

Alquist. Domain, I'm going to get the best room ready for Miss Glory.

Domain. Wait a moment. I'm afraid that—that Miss Glory hasn't finished speaking.

Helena. No. I haven't. Unless you close my lips by force.

Dr. Gall. Harry, don't you dare.

Helena. Thank you. I knew that you'd protect me.

Domain. Excuse me, Miss Glory, but I suppose you think you're talking to Robots?

Helena [*startled*]. Of course.

Domain. I'm sorry. These gentlemen are human beings just like us. Like the whole of Europe.

Helena [*to the others*]. You're not Robots?

Berman [*with a guffaw*]. God forbid.

So it is a fine liberal sentiment which brings Helena to the island. Revealed as an activist, she asks Domain whether he will allow her to address the Robots. After all, her intentions are clear—to turn the Robots into dissidents who claim their civil rights and a union wage. Domain, recalling a dreary succession of preachers, prophets, missionaries and anarchists who have come to the island to proclaim their message, not only agrees to let Helena address the Robots but even offers to supply a captive audience of thousands of them in the Robot warehouse. Of course, there is a certain element of curiosity concerning the aim of Helena's organization (the Humanity League) . . .

Fabry. Pardon me. But kindly tell me what is the real aim of your League —the—the Humanity League.

Helena. Its real purpose is to—to protect the Robots—and—and ensure good treatment for them.

Fabry. Not a bad object, either. A machine has to be treated properly. Upon my soul, I approve of that. I don't like damaged articles. Please, Miss Glory, enroll us all as contributing, as regular, as foundation, members of your League.

Helena. No, you don't understand me. What we really want is to—to liberate the Robots.

Helman. How do you propose to do that?

Helena. They are to be—to be dealt with like human beings.

There are some interesting commercial implications in adding Robots to the international labor force. These additions are in nontrivial quantities—for example five hundred thousand Robots (the tropical variety) have just been added to (or have just displaced) Argentine corn growers. Domain details some of these implications in what is patently a sales pitch but which he seems—as is too often the case with General Managers—to believe:

Domain. . . . But in ten years Rossum's Universal Robots will produce so much corn, so much cloth, so much everything, that things will be practically without price. Everyone will take as much as he wants. There'll be no poverty. Yes, there'll be unemployed. But, then, there won't be any employment. Everything will be done by living machines. The Robots will clothe and feed us. The Robots will make bricks and build houses for us. The Robots will keep our accounts and sweep our stairs. There'll be no employment, but everybody will be free from worry, and liberated from the degradation of labor. Everybody will live only to perfect himself.

Helena. [*standing up*]. Will he?

Domain. Of course. It's bound to happen. There may perhaps be terrible doings first, Miss Glory. That simply can't be avoided. But, then, the servitude of man to man and the enslavement of man to matter will cease. The Robots will wash the feet of the beggar and prepare a bed for him in his own house. Nobody will get bread at the price of life and hatred. There'll be no artisans, no clerks, no hewers of coal and minders of other men's machines.

Helena is not particularly interested in a joint invitation to lunch; there is something else on her mind . . .

Helena.   Perhaps it's silly of me, but—why do you manufacture female Robots, when—when——

Domain.   When—hm—sex means nothing to them?

Helena.   Yes.

Domain.   There's a certain demand for them, you see. Servants, saleswomen, clerks. People are used to it.

Helena.   But—but, tell me, are the Robots, male and female—mutually —altogether——

Domain.   Altogether indifferent to each other, Miss Glory. There's no sign of any affection between them.

Helena.   Oh, that's terrible.

Domain.   Why?

Helena.   It's so—so unnatural. One doesn't know whether to be disgusted, or whether to hate them, or perhaps——

Domain.   To pity them.

[Well, these neuter relations are not entirely unnatural perhaps. Not that there are no variances to be found in the area of robot romance, as may be observed in Karl Bruckner's *The Hour of the Robots.*]

In Act II, the time is five years later, Helena and Domain are married, still stuck on that island, and (as the ad men say) robotwise things have gone downhill. Helena puts it succinctly:

Helena . . .   And you see, Harry, for all these five years I've not lost this— this anxiety, and you've never felt the least misgiving—not even when everything went wrong.

Domain.   What went wrong?

Helena.   Your plans, Harry. When, for example, the workmen struck against the Robots and smashed them up, and when the people gave the Robots firearms against the rebels and the Robots killed so many people. And then when the Governments turned the Robots into soldiers and there were so many wars, and all that.

It might be thought that this sort of activity would be immaterial so far as robots are concerned. But it seems that turning robots into soldiers and sending them off to war has on them the same sort of dreary effect it has upon humans. To make matters worse, the robots have become still more sophisticated and are, in their robot way, aware of the man-robot relationship—an embittering situation. As the robot Radius puts it to Helena, at one point:

Radius. Send me to the stamping mill.

Helena. I am sorry that they are going to kill you. Why weren't you more careful?

Radius. I won't work for you. Put me into the stamping mill.

Helena. Why do you hate us?

Radius. You are not like the Robots. You are not as skillful as the Robots. The Robots can do everything. You only give orders. You talk more than is necessary.

Helena. That's foolish, Radius. Tell me, has anyone upset you? I should so much like you to understand me.

Radius. You do nothing but talk.

Helena. Doctor Gall gave you a larger brain than the rest, larger than ours, the largest in the world. You are not like the other Robots, Radius. You understand me perfectly.

Radius. I don't want any master. I know everything for myself.

Helena. That's why I had you put into the library, so that you could read everything, understand everything, and then—Oh, Radius, I wanted you to show the whole world that the Robots were our equals. That's what I wanted of you.

Radius. I don't want any master. I want to be master over others.

Helena. I'm sure they'd put you in charge of many Robots, Radius. You would be a teacher of the Robots.

Radius. I want to be master over people.

Helena. You have gone mad.

Radius. You can put me into the stamping mill.

Helena. Do you suppose that we're frightened of such a madman as you? [*sits down at the table and writes a note.*] No, not a bit. Radius, give this note to Mr. Domain. It is to ask them not to take you to the stamping mill. [*standing up.*] How you hate us. Why does nothing in the world please you?

Radius. I can do everything.

Alas, Robots, it seems, can do all things but one. They send their armed divisions around the world, defeat the humans, and—as the humans have always hitherto done to each other—undertake a program of extermination of humans. This is done with such meticulous efficiency that, at the end of the play, only one human has been left alive—Alquist, one of the production managers at the Robot-producing factory. It turns out that the one thing Robots cannot do is produce more Robots. And in a major blunder they neglect to keep alive any humans who *do* know how to produce Robots.

The play ends with a tantalizing development: It may be that Robots have been made so human-like that they may in fact be humanized—and thus able to reproduce themselves in the old human way. (Should this happen, one wonders whether the whole cycle would be repeated again ... and again ...)

REFERENCES

Delgado, J. M. R. (1969), *Physical Control of the Mind: Toward a Psychocivilized Society*. Harper & Row.

Good, I. J. (1965), Speculations concerning the first ultra intelligent machine, *Advances in Computers* **6**, eds. F. L. Alt and M. Rubinoff. Academic Press.

Hayes, P. J. (1970), Robotologic, *Machine Intelligence* **5**, 533–554.

Scriven, M. (1960), "The compleat robot: a prolegomena to androidology," *Dimensions of Mind*, ed. S. Hook. New York: NYU Press.

12 *The Desk Set:*
man vs. machine—the last victory

Speaking of the career women in the modern business corporation, the editors of *Fortune* wrote:

> The male is the name on the door, the hat on the coat rack, and the smoke in the corner room. But the male is not the office. The office is the competent woman at the other end of his buzzer, the two young ladies chanting his name monotonously into the mouthpieces of a kind of gutta-percha halter, the four girls in the glass coop pecking out his initials with pink fingernails on the keyboards of four voluble machines, the half dozen assorted skirts whisking through the filling cases of his correspondence, and the elegant miss in the reception room, recognizing his friends and disposing of his antipathies with the pleased voice and impersonal eye of a presidential consort.

In his incisive study of the middle class, *White Collar*, C. Wright Mills found himself musing over the personnel structure of the crew that serves the modern corporation ⌊Chapter 9: The Enormous File⌋. A fragment of the structure—the top managerial cadre—has a constantly automatizing influence upon the structure beneath. This lower structure is laced into a hierarchy by the managers, and position in the hierarchy is determined not by ability or skill but by the authority of the managers. The cost reduction drive of management that has led to automatizing in the past now leads to automation. On the assembly lines the lathes and tool cutting devices are placed under computer control. In the white collar hierarchies the jobs and tasks are subdivided and tightly specified and carefully inter-related; they then are susceptible to programming and can be relegated to the computer. Costs decrease and efficiency grows.

The final irony in the managerial decree that computers shall ascend in the corporate structure is that the managerial class must itself, finally, be displaced by computers. Top level decisions of the past—the dispositions of tanker fleets, strategies of corporate conglomeration, the weighing of a spectrum of inventories against ambient markets—are properly made with mathematical techniques beyond the ken of the current captains of industry. The intuitions of the past must yield to the algorithms of the present.

In the beginning, when the computer was first gaining a toehold in the corporate structure, programming errors were rife and vacuum tubes not always dependable, it seems that the electronic oracle was occasionally a figure of fun in whose oafish strength lay the merest hint of menace —something like Lenny, in *Of Mice and Men*. The computer had to be rated against *Fortune's* intelligent but vulnerable career women who crewed the corporate craft. A fragment of the crew is examined in the play *The Desk Set*, by William Marchant,* produced on Broadway in 1955. (This was the year after the first Univac for business data processing was installed at the General Electric Appliance Division.) At that time the computers which were being installed for business applications were intended for the most prevalent routine tasks. The subtleties of which computers were capable were either unrealized in the Olympian levels of the corporate cannery or—if they were—the corporate chiefs brooded silently over the prospect of the coming ascendency of electronic decisions. So the role into which Marchant cast a computer in *The Desk Set* was a serviceable dramatic device but premature by more than a decade as a representation of an all-purpose information processing device.

The Desk Set maps the intrusion of a computer into the operations of a television-broadcasting company. Typically enough the machine is to

---

* William Marchant. *The Desk Set*. Samuel French, Inc. New York. Copyright © William Marchant, 1955, 1956. Excerpts of the play appearing in this chapter are reprinted by permission of International Famous Agency.

process the accounting and payroll operations of the company. But—atypically—the machine is intended to intervene into the operations of the Reference Department, the staff of which consists of four women *à la* the *Fortune* editorial view. (One of the four—Bunny Watson—is a woman of unusual wit and intelligence: Any computer assuming the functions of the Department would presumably displace *her*, and so the issue is joined.)

Scouting the territory in advance, an operations research type—Richard Sumner—drifts into the Reference Department and uses a tape measure to verify that the Department actually has enough space to encompass the machine. He goes about this task in an uncommunicative, supercilious way ("He looks like one of the men who's just suddenly switched to vodka"). Then, having gauged the physical capacity of the Reference Department, he undertakes to gauge its intellectual capacity. But that occurs in round two. A bit of exploratory sparring takes place first. Sumner asks to speak to Bunny Watson in private, and she asks, just what's going on?

Richard. (*Sits Right.*)   Well, Miss Watson, I didn't want to say anything in front of your staff, because whenever I mention what I do everybody is thrown into a panic—

Bunny.   Good heavens—what do you do?

Richard.   I'm a methods engineer.

Bunny.   Is that anything like an efficiency expert?

Richard. (*Frowns.*)   That term is a bit obsolete.

Bunny.   Forgive me. I'm so sorry. I'm the old-fashioned type. I thought I knew everyone in the building, but I haven't seen you around the building before.

Richard.   I've only been here a few months—Just wandering about—

Bunny.   Oh, I see—sort of a migratory engineer—

Richard.   Yes, but I'll be in here for the next few weeks.

Bunny.   Tell me, Mr. Sumner—what would a methods engineer be doing in our little iron lung?

Richard.   You'd be surprised how a bit of scientific application can improve the work-man-hour relationship.

Bunny. (*Eyes him.*)   Uh-huh. Fascinating.

Richard.   And time, as they say, is money—

Bunny.   Yes, so I've heard.

Sumner, however, remains coy about his exact intentions. But Bunny later gets a feeling for the shape of things to come; one of her supervisors identifies Sumner:

. . . He's the boy responsible for that shakeup down in Payroll and Accounting. (*Sits chair Right.*)

Bunny.   He's the one.

Abe.   Yes. He installed one of those electronic brains down there and half the department disappeared.

So there you have it. If the machine can do 100 man-hours of work in two seconds, there's not much point in having 100 men standing about when a little machine could be ticking away in their place. At $600 per hour, two seconds of work by the computer costs well under one dollar; at $4 per hour the work of 100 men costs $400. Small wonder that half the department disappeared! In fact, at the next confrontation between Bunny Watson and Sumner, he learns that she has seen a demonstration by the computer and asks what she thinks of it:

Richard.   Did you see it translate from the Russian and Chinese?

Bunny.   I saw it do everything. It's kind of spooky.

Richard.   It does give you the feeling that maybe—just maybe—that people are a little bit outmoded.

Bunny.   Yes, I wouldn't be a bit surprised if they stopped making them—

Bunny asks how the personnel in Payroll and Accounting felt about competition from the computer:

Richard.   Oh, you get a lot of resistance to anything as new as this.

Bunny.   Well, I don't think I'll worry about it—that machine couldn't do the work I do.

Richard.   (He nods contradictingly.) Oh yes, *it* could.

Bunny.   Well, this office is different, Mr. Sumner—we don't have the space for a lot of cross-references, you see; so it has to rely pretty much on the good memories of the people who work here. And I'd match my memory against that machine's any day.

Richard. That's a fairly idle boast, isn't it?

Bunny. Is it?

Sumner then undertakes his little exercise in personality assessment and we begin to get a measure of the calibre of Bunny Watson's competence:

Richard. I have a personality questionnaire here that several of the other department heads have answered. These things often seem a little silly, but you'd be amazed at what it tells us about general intelligence, adaptability, deductive powers—and it may be a bit of a tease for your memory—

Bunny. Oh, a tease?

Richard. Just answer whatever comes into your head—I mean don't dwell on the questions.

Bunny. Oh, no.

Richard. Often when we meet people for the first time, some physical characteristic strikes us. What is the first thing you notice in a person?

Bunny. Whether the person is male or female.

Richard. (Richard *makes a note on his questionnaire.*) Now this is a little mathematical problem. "A train started out at Grand Central with seventeen passengers aboard and a crew of nine. At 125th Street four got off and nine got on. At White Plains, three got off and one got on. At Chappaqua, nine got off and four got on, and at each successive stop thereafter, nobody got off and nobody got on, until the train reached its next to its last stop, where five people got off and one got on. Then it reached the terminal."

Bunny. Oh, that's easy. Eleven passengers and a crew of nine.

Richard. That's not the question.

Bunny. Oh.

Richard. How many people got off at Chappaqua?

Bunny. Nine.

Richard. That's correct. How did you happen to get that?

Bunny. Spooky, isn't it? Do you notice there are also nine letters in Chappaqua?

Richard. Are you accustomed to associating words with the number of letters they contain?

Bunny. I associate many things with many things.

Richard. I see.

Bunny. Aren't you going to ask me how many people got off at White Plains?—Three.

Richard. But there are ten letters in White Plains.

Bunny. No—eleven.

Richard. I stand corrected.

Bunny. I've only ever been to White Plains three times in my whole life.

Richard. Suppose you had only been there twice?

Bunny. But I wasn't. I was there three times.

Richard. Very well. We'll go on to something else.

Bunny. Ask me how many people got on at Croton Falls.

Richard. There is no Croton Falls mentioned in the question.

Bunny. No, but it's the next to the last stop on that line, anyway.

Richard. Do you notice anything unusual about the following sentence: "Able Was I Ere I Saw Elba"?

Bunny. No, but I doubt that Napoleon ever said anything like that.
(*Evidently pleased with this answer, he makes a hurried notation on a piece of paper.*)
Unless you mean it's because it's spelled the same way backwards and forwards, is that what you mean?
(*And he is obliged to erase what he has written.*) What do they call it, a palindrome?

Richard. I really don't know what they call it.

Bunny. I know another: Madam, I'm Adam. (*She laughs slightly.*)

Richard. (*He glances through his papers, searching for that one tricky question that she will be unable to answer.*) Here are three telephone numbers, which I will repeat only once. You try to repeat them after me. Ready?

Bunny. Yes—

Richard. Plaza 6–3391—Murray Hill 1–1051 and Plaza 6–3931.

Bunny. Plaza 6–3391—Murray Hill 1–1051—and Plaza 6–3931.

Richard. (*Thoroughly irritated.*) Now I would like you to explain to me how you got them all correct.

Bunny. The first is Plaza 6—with the year of the bank failure reversed. And the second is Murray Hill 1 with fifteen years before the date of the Norman Conquest. And the last Plaza 6 was the same as the first, with the third and fourth numbers transposed. Except there's something terribly wrong with that question.

Richard. Really?

Bunny. I don't think there is any Plaza 6 exchange.

Richard. Now before asking you the next question, I must advise you that it contains a trick. And in order to see into the trick, I give you two words of advice: Never assume.

Bunny. Never assume?

Richard. Ready? "A detective broke into an apartment and found Harry and Grace lying on the floor, dead. Beside them was a small pool of water and some fragments of broken glass. Above them, on a sofa, looking down at them, was a pet cat, its back arched. The detective concluded, without further investigation, that the victims had died of strangulation. How was this conclusion possible?"

Bunny. (*After a moment.*)   Never assume, hmmmmm?

Richard. Never assume.

Bunny. Well the only thing I'm assuming—*oh!* Were Harry and Grace— no, that's silly. Were Harry and Grace—goldfish?

Richard. (*Snaps notebook shut.*) Well—I think we'll just abandon this, now.

Bunny. Oh, no! I'm having fun.

Richard. That wasn't quite the point of it.

Bunny. Well, what's my grade?

Richard. (*Moving out into outer office.*) We don't grade them.

Bunny. (*Following him every step of the way.*)   Then why give the test?

Richard. We have a general classification table with personality categories. Such as—Slow—Alert—Totally Receptive and Total Recall. (*He heads for the door Right.*)

Bunny. And how do you classify me?

Richard. (*Turns back to* Bunny.) I never had anybody quite like you before. We have an extreme classification I've never used, but it has to be applied to you.

Bunny.   What is it?

Richard.   FREAK! *(And he's out the door.)*

(Bunny watches him go thoughtfully—turns and regards the sign: THINK—)

Sumner does not get away scot free with this impertinence. He has another encounter with Bunny Watson in Act III, in which he is, this time, drawn up in full battle array, like the French knights at Agincourt, the great armored computer at the ready and his faithful programmer-retainer at his side. Bunny Watson and her little corps have their intellectual longbows drawn, and the confrontation begins with a query being put to the computer: What's the annual damage done to American forests by the spruce bud worm? One of Bunny Watson's staff, with a commendable sense of fair play, feels this is too stiff a test of strength:

Peg.   Oh, don't do that! You'll be here until tomorrow! I had three folders *this* thick on it. I had to borrow an adding machine to count up all the damage he did in California alone. It's one hundred and thirty-eight million dollars.

(Miss Warriner has been throwing switches, setting dials, etc., and now the roll of tape moves slightly, the machine makes a rumbling noise and then a sigh, and Miss Warriner turns.)

Warriner.   Here's your answer. One hundred thirty-eight million, four hundred sixty-four dollars and seventy-five cents.

(There is a stunned silence. The Girls look at one another. Bunny shrugs, looks in bewilderment to Peg.)

And while the ladies are still reeling from this display of instant knowledge, the mail boy comes in and hands them, each and every one, a pink slip! Their reaction to being fired is one of stunned despair, but in the light of the just completed electronic performance, the pink slip strikes them as somehow understandable. And yet . . .

Peg.   No matter how you prepare yourself, it's always a blow.

Sadel.   There goes ten years of seniority—Well, now that I've got it I feel better—at least I can stop worrying about the whole thing.

> *Ruthie. (Looks at check.)* Two weeks' pay—(*Tries to smile.*) How long
> does it take before you start collecting your unemployment insurance?
> *Sadel.* Two weeks—I looked it up.

But shortly later, as the question-and-answer routine of the day gets into
high gear, the mechanical oracle is revealed as having feet of clay (and a
brain to match). Asked

i) Whether the King of the Watusi drives a car,
ii) for information on Corfu, and
iii) for the total weight of the earth,

the computer clumsily replies with (i) a review of the movie *King Solo-
mon's Mines*, (ii) the eighty stanzas of *Curfew Shall Not Ring Tonight*,
and (iii) a return question—a notable idiocy—"WITH OR WITHOUT
PEOPLE?" Moreover, in between, it suffers mechanical failure, but is
put right by Bunny Watson using nothing more than a hair pin.

One might wonder at this point how *gauche* can a computer be? Alas,
the end is not in sight: That silly computer sent a pink slip to each
employee in the company (and one to the president). So the reference
staff has not really been fired after all, and we have a third act finale
ending on the classical upbeat—the undeniable prospect of symbiosis
(roughly speaking) between the reference staff and the machine. In a
flat confrontation between man (or woman, rather) and machine,
man comes out on top—an easy and graceful winner.

One looks back at Marchant's presentation with a kind of nostalgia.
Those were the wonderful days of the vacuum tube, before the transistor held sway. Man was still the victor. It's like thinking about the
Green Bay Packers after one of their bad seasons: There were times, in
the old days, when they were great.

REFERENCES

Armstrong, Sir W. (1970), A lunch-time look at CS computing, *Computer
Bulletin* **14**, 224–226.

Myers, C. A. (1968), *The Impact of Computers on Management*. MIT Press.

Sanders, D. H., ed. (1970), *Computers and Management*. McGraw-Hill.

Shepard, J. M. (1971), *Automation and Alienation*. MIT Press.

Svensson, C. (1970), Banking applications, *Computer Bulletin* **14**, 309–317.

Thurston, P. H. (1962), Who should control information systems? *Harvard Business Review* **40**, 135–139.

Walker, C. R. (1968), *Technology, Industry, and Man*. McGraw-Hill.

The Billion Dollar Brain:
the computer as espionage agent

In Graham Greene's *Our Man in Havana* a retiring British merchant sells vacuum cleaners in Havana until one day he is importuned by a notably inept British intelligence service to become one of their agents. Preferring to avoid the unpatriotic aspect and moved by the prospect of financial gain, Our Man finds himself acting as agent. At the insistence of London, he at last begins drafting reports—with no information to embody them—and joyfully discovers that he has a flair for fiction. The reports build in volume, effusions of fantasy detailing the efforts of his (artfully invented) stable of sub-agents, the salaries for whom London benignly supplies (to Our Man's enjoyment).

A parallel circumstance provides the theme for Len Deighton's *The Billion Dollar Brain* in which a wealthy Texas oil man has set up a private international army and a spy network to go with it. As with the larger petroleum corporations today, the logistics of this army are a strictly computer-controlled affair. And so is the handling of the spy network. The computer collates all intelligence reports, makes a unified analysis of the situation in the field, calculates an optimal strategy, and automatically issues instructions to the principal agents. One of these agents, a key operative in the Baltic zone, named Harvey Newbegin, explains to an old friend (who happens to be a British intelligence agent) how the system works:

. . . "All our operations are programmed on electronic machines. Each stage is recorded on a tape machine and each operator reports the end

of each stage to that machine and the machine will—providing all
the agents on that scheme have also reported in—tell you the next
stage."

"You mean you're working for a calculating machine?"

"We call it the Brain," said Harvey. "That's how we can be so sure
that no slip-ups occur. The machine correlates the reports of all the agents
and then relays the next set of instructions. Each agent has a telephone
number. He phones that number and obeys the recorded instructions he
receives. *

This claim about no slip-ups is false, as Harvey himself well knows: He
has adopted a ploy roughly equivalent to that used by Our Man in
Havana. The details of Harvey's ruse are unraveled by the British agent
(without aid of computer), who later informs the Texas oil man about this
small defect in the organization:

. . .   "Newbegin has been feeding you phantom agents for a long time.
He operates a swindle with your money. He pays a package of money
to one of your agents, who then passes it on to a second real agent who
passes it on to a third agent who just happens to be Harvey Newbegin
dressed up in fancy disguise. Harvey then puts the money in the bank
for himself. He probably does that for every network to which he has
access. The rest of the network is just a lot of fancy paper work."

It may be thought that a personal computer installation could hardly be
adequate to cope with the responsibilities which face this one, but (as
Harvey points out) it turns out that the cost of the installation is over a
billion dollars, and, as for the equipment itself, Harvey claims: " . . . It's
the most complex computer in existence today. The machines in this
building cost over a hundred million dollars to develop and the machine
equipment and construction . . . nearly as much again."

And what does one get at this price?

---

* This and the two excerpts following are reprinted by permission of G. P.
Putnam's Sons from *The Billion Dollar Brain* by Len Deighton. Copyright ©
1966 by Len Deighton.

"I don't want to bore you," Harvey said, "but you should understand that these heaps of wire can practically think—linear programming—which means that instead of going through all the alternatives they have a hunch which is the right one. What's more, almost none of them work by binary notation—the normal method for computers—because that's just yes/no stuff. (If you can only store yesses and noes it takes seven punch holes to record the number ninety-nine.) These machines use tiny chips of ceramic which store electricity. They store any amount from one to nine. That's why—for what it does—this whole setup is so small."

If private espionage organizations can enjoy heaps of wires that practically think, it is interesting to conjecture about the heaps that are used in the service of the state. In the absence of official specifications issued by the Central Intelligence Agency we settle for an offhand description of some of CIA's machinery offered by the director in William Garner's *The Us or Them War*:

. . . STARCOM stands for Strategic and Tactical Assessment and Review Computer. It has one great advantage over the rest of us. It knows only what we tell it, but it knows as much as all of us put together: the entire U.S. security, defense and information services. Also, it never forgets anything, and we do.

"It can answer a pretty comprehensive range of questions on security and defense matters. Or, more exactly, given a choice of answers, it rates them in order of probability, which is the way most human beings think. Only STARCOM does it a hell of a lot faster than human beings, and without missing any tricks."*

If the Americans have a relatively omniscient computer to map strategy and safeguard the Republic, can the Russians be far behind? Not really. In fact, they may be a pace or two ahead. In Garner's story, a key American project seems to involve *penetrating* the Russian version of STARCOM. (Garner fails to tell us the name of the Russian version, and in the event that he might be contemplating a sequel, we suggest COMPSYMP—for Computer Synthesis and Amplification—or

---

* William Garner. *The Us or Them War*. G. P. Putnam's Sons. Reprinted by permission.

COMINTERN—for Computer Integration, Evaluation, Reassessment and Nullification.) The penetration project is only partly successful—as seems to be frequently the case with CIA projects abroad—but still it is comforting to know that our intelligence agencies undertake this type of enterprise. In their *The Invisible Government*, Wise and Ross in 1964 estimated the staff of the CIA as numbering about 200,000 people. Applying Parkinson's Law and taking into account the national budget of 1964 with the current budget, the present staff of the CIA is probably about 400,000.

So it may be that if a billion dollars worth of computer installations is necessary to keep track of the stable of agents described by Len Deighton, a more hefty installation must be ticking away in one of the subbasements in Langley, Virginia. And there are current intentions to install a counterpart of STARCOM for domestic purposes. The envisioned National Data Center would encompass all of the information presently fragmented among many federal agencies and probably various state agencies. The idea of a national data center was proposed in 1965 by a committee of the Social Science Research Council to aid in the study of social and economic problems. Demographic aspects of disease, unemployment, urban decay, and environmental design could be more powerfully researched with the enormous reservoir of data which such a center could make available. Those who support the data bank concept point out that many federal agencies (Internal Revenue, Social Security Administration, Census Bureau, ...) already collect data of various kinds related to individual citizens; so the data center would not be doing anything new, it would simply be improving access to the total accumulation of information.

There are, however, implications regarding the invasion of privacy which the data bank poses. These implications are underlined by the abuses observed in the operation of private credit-rating bureaus. Accordingly, in 1966 the House Government Operations Committee's Special Subcommittee on Invasion of Privacy held hearings on the question. One of the witnesses before the Committee, Vance Packard (author of *The Naked Society*), with Orwell's *1984* obviously in mind, said: "My hunch is that Big Brother, if he ever comes to these United States, may turn out to be not a greedy power seeker, but rather a relentless bureaucrat obsessed with efficiency."

The Committee later issued a report recommending that the design of a national data center should provide technical safeguards against misuse or unauthorized access to the data, and that the data itself be maintained in the aggregate rather than in the form of information identifiable with particular persons. It also suggested that a new agency be set up to maintain and operate such a center, rather than lodge the center in an existing federal agency—presumably this would tend to reduce the likelihood of political exploitation of the center.

In March 1967 the Senate Committee on the Judiciary's Subcommittee on Administrative Practice and Procedure held hearings on "Computer Privacy." Part of the testimony involved a report by the Task Force on the Storage of and Access to Government Statistics, headed by Carl Kaysen (director of the Institute for Advanced Study, Princeton). The report led off with some observations on the Government's statistical operations:

> . . . As it is presently operated, the statistical system is both inadequate—in the sense of failing to do things that should and could be done, and inefficient—in the sense of not doing what it does at minimum cost . . .

After buttressing this mild indictment with substantial argument, the report went on to recommend a National Data Center, which would be

1) To establish and maintain an inventory of all available data in the relevant categories in the Federal System.
2) To set and enforce uniform disclosure standards so that the legal requirement of confidentiality can be met with no unnecessary sacrifice of analytically useful information.
3) Similarly, in cooperation with the state and local government units, to perform similar tasks . . .
4) To assemble centrally the data from all these sources . . .
5) In cooperation with users in and out of government and collection agencies, to set the standards for further collection efforts . . .

To clear the air, another witness, C. J. Zwick (Assistant Director, Bureau of the Budget) gave the current status of the situation by stating that " . . . First, no such center has been organized, and further, that the administration will not undertake to create one without first submitting to the Congress specific plans for its review and approval." In general, Government witnesses saw little to fear in the way of invasion of privacy and seemed to view the data bank as being realizable as a sort of informational Fort Knox, located somewhere in Washington, D.C., where the inviolability of the data would be a consequence of its storage form (magnetic tape). Another witness, Prof. Arthur R. Miller (University of Michigan) was dubious about this point of view, and stated:

> . . . It may be true that it will be harder to get at information stored in a computerized data center—in the parlance of the wiretapping game, the cost per unit of dirt may go up—but the amount of dirt per unit that a successful attempt at snooping will yield will be sharply increased because of the centralized quality of the information. Furthermore, we have no idea today—absolutely no idea—of the ways in which the genius of modern technology will be used to reduce the cost of improperly gaining access to a center.

Still another witness, Lawrence Speiser (director of the Washington office of the American Civil Liberties Union) saw the problem in the following light:

> . . . The establishment of a Federal data center would create the machinery for the maintenance of personal dossiers on a great many Americans— a concept odious to a free society. There is no dispute about this, even from the proponents of the data bank. They have insisted all along that in order for the statistical data stored in the data center to be of value, an ultimate key must be kept somewhere so that the human beings involved can be identified.

> . . . It is not necessary to spell out to this committee the palpable dangers in the Government having a personal dossier on millions of its citizens. It should only be noted that not all the danger relates to abuse of a malicious nature by one seeking political power or other patently unworthy ends. The information stored in the bank may be a cause of harm even in high-principled hands. Unfortunately, the great bulk of information about an

individual is not gathered as a result of inquiries by skilled Government investigators. Rather, it is often acquired by Government employees of poor judgment, by private agencies, credit unions, insurance companies and businesses . . . Once an unreliable bit of information makes its way into a file, it forms an indelible mark on a person's record.

This was not the first time that the ACLU had addressed itself to the problem of data banks. In May 1970 the ACLU Foundation filed suit in the Federal District Court (Washington) to stop the United States Army from collecting information on politically dissident individuals and organizations. The suit claimed that "anonymous informers, the FBI and state and local police gather and feed to the Army information on virtually all political protest occurring anywhere within the United States." In a memorandum later filed with the Court, the ACLU also claimed that the Army's domestic intelligence program "involves the conduct of undercover operations by military agents within the civilian community, the maintenance of over a dozen regional and national records centers on political protests, and the distribution to military units and to federal agencies of hundreds of 'identification lists' describing individuals and organizations who have objected to governmental policies and social conditions."

The suit was dismissed by District Judge George L. Hart, Jr., who declared that the Army was not "doing anything newspapers are not doing . . . keeping information in their morgues" [*Computerworld*, May 6, 1970], to which the ACLU counsel replied: "Newspapers don't have guns and don't have jails. Nobody is afraid that someday the news services are going to sweep into town and arrest the troublemakers." Judge Hart refused to let the ACLU present witnesses at the hearing. Among these, according to *Computerworld*, was the man who set up "the New Left desk of the Counter-Intelligence Analysis Division (CIAD) at the Pentagon. He reported that he had access to the CIAD's computer-indexed microfilmed data bank which contained information on 3000 to 5000 civilians and over 300 organizations."

In February and March, 1971, the Senate Subcommittee on Constitutional Rights held hearings on Computers, Data Banks, and the Bill of Rights. That part of the testimony that related to the Army mounting intelligence operations against Americans on home ground is an odd mixture of George Orwell and Gilbert & Sullivan. And it can all be summed up in the words of Walt Kelly's Pogo:

"We have met the enemy, and they is us."

REFERENCES

Bigelow, R. P. (1967), Legal and security issues posed by computer utilities, *Harvard Business Review* **45**, 150.

Hoffman, L. J. (1969), Computers and privacy: a survey, *Computing Surveys* **1**, 85.

Miller, A. R. (1971), *The Assault on Privacy: Computers, Data Banks and Dossiers*. University of Michigan Press.

Westin, A. (1967), *Privacy and Freedom*. New York: Atheneum.

See also:

Symposium—computers, data banks, and individual privacy, *Minnesota Law Review* **53**, (1968).

Plot thickens in plotting program "theft," *Datamation*, (April 15, 1971).

Army files on lawful civilian political activity, *Computerworld*, (February 11, 1970), 6–7.

Privacy, security, and a free America, a speech by Congressman Frank Horton, entered by Congressman Cornelius E. Gallagher in the *Congressional Record* (Sept. 23, 1970).

FBI to computerize rap file; no safeguards planned, *Computerworld* (Sept. 30, 1970); a responding letter to the editor, captioned "FBI's Hoover criticizes CW's NCIC coverage" by J. Edgar Hoover; and the editorial reply, "The FBI missed the point, *Computerworld* (Oct. 28, 1970).

Tom Wicker. Raw material for the snoopers, *New York Times* (Feb. 16, 1971).

Senator Sam J. Erwin, Jr. Announcement of hearings on computers, data banks, and the bill of rights, *Congressional Record* **117** (Feb. 8, 1971).

14 *The Hour of the Robots:* the computer as lover

It is not surprising to encounter the proposal that science should be abandoned, at least for the time being. This solution appeals especially to those who are fitted by temperament to other ways of life. Some relief might be obtained if we could divert mankind into a revival of the arts or religion or even of that petty quarreling which we now look back upon as a life of peace. Such a program resembles the decision of the citizens of Samuel Butler's *Erewhon*, where the instruments and products of science were put into museums—as vestiges of a stage in the evolution of human culture which did not survive. But not everyone is willing to defend a position of stubborn "not knowing." There is no virtue in ignorance for its own sake.*

B. F. Skinner
Science and Human Behavior

. . . .

Faced with the question of imparting intelligence to machines, man finds himself in the disheartening position of having apparently failed in the attempt to impart knowledge to man. The growing disenchantment that society exhibits toward the schools and universities—even the studied (and occasionally strenuous) rejection by the young—stems perhaps from a principal cause: The reluctance of the educational regime to assume responsibility for the direction and application of the science and tech-

---

* From B. F. Skinner, *Science and Human Behavior*, Copyright 1953, The Macmillan Co. Reprinted by permission.

nology which it teaches. Late in the twentieth century man finds himself in an appalling position. Science and technology have placed in the hands of the military establishment the means for the obliteration of human life on a global scale, justifying their provision of this terrible power with the claim that the responsibility lies elsewhere and sometimes disdaining any justification whatsoever. The underlying attitude that supports this behaviorism seems to parallel, in a striking way, the brilliant cynicism of Bernard Shaw's wealthy munitions maker, Lord Undershaft:*

Lomax [*leniently*]. Well, the more destructive war becomes, the sooner it will be abolishēd, eh?

Undershaft. Not at all. The more destructive war becomes the more fascinating we find it. No, Mr. Lomax: I am obliged to you for making the usual excuse for my trade; but I am not ashamed for it. I am not one of those men who keep their morals and their business in watertight compartments. All the spare money my trade rivals spend on hospitals, cathedrals, and other receptacles for conscience money, I devote to experiments and researches in improved methods of destroying life and property. I have always done so, and I always shall. Therefore your Christmas card moralities of peace on earth and goodwill among men are of no use to me. Your Christianity, which enjoins you to resist not evil, and to turn the other cheek, would make me a bankrupt. My morality—my religion—must have a place for cannons and torpedoes in it.

For a stark display of Undershaftmanship on the part of the scientific establishment, we might consider the recommendation of the Interim Committee appointed by (then President) Truman in 1945. The question to which the Committee addressed itself was: Should the newly developed atomic bomb be demonstrated to the Japanese by exploding it over an uninhabited island or ruthlessly against an unwarned Japanese population center? The Committee (consisting of President James B. Conant of Harvard University, and others) asked the advice of a Scientific Advisory Panel, consisting of four physicists: E. O. Lawrence of the

---

* From Shaw's *Major Barbara*, about 1906. See *Six Plays By Bernard Shaw*. Dodd, Mead & Co, New York, 1945. Reprinted by permission of the Society of Authors on behalf of the Shaw Estate.

Berkeley Radiation Laboratory, Arthur Compton of the Chicago Metallurgical Laboratory, Enrico Fermi of the University of Chicago, and J. R. Oppenheimer of the Los Alamos Atomic Laboratory. According to Philip Stern's synthesis of the Oppenheimer case*:

> The four ultimately concluded that they could "see no acceptable alternative to direct military use" of the bomb. They ended their report on a modest note: Even though as nuclear scientists they had had special opportunity to think about the implications of atomic energy, they could claim no "special competence in solving the political, social and military problems which are represented by the advent of atomic power."

A mere two atomic bombs devastated two cities, incinerated 150,000 people and injured 50,000 more. What was the attitude of the scientific establishment to the idea of a hydrogen bomb—a weapon 1000 times more powerful than an atomic bomb? The answer is not entirely clear. The physicist Edward Teller, an important figure in the development of the hydrogen bomb (as well as the atomic bomb) has said†:

> To the best of my recollection before we got to Los Alamos we had all of us considerable hopes that the thermonuclear bomb can be constructed.

But, on the other hand, he also said:

> . . . on some visits when Bethe came there, he looked the program over someway [sic] critically and quite frankly he said he wished the thing would not work.

Feelings on the matter were mixed and often shifted with time or circumstance. But the one compelling conclusion that may be drawn from a

---

* Philip M. Stern. *The Oppenheimer Case: Security on Trial.* Harper & Row. New York, 1969.

† United States Atomic Energy Commission. *In the Matter of J. Robert Oppenheimer.* Transcript of Hearing before Personnel Security Board. Government Printing Office, Washington, DC. 1954. [Usually refered to as the Gray Report, after the chairman of the Security Board, Gordon Gray.] See p. 711.

reading of the nuclear bomb development is that there was never a dearth of scientists ready to research and produce weapons of mass destruction. In Teller's words, the scientist's task is only to study "the laws of nature" but "it is *not* the scientist's job to determine whether a hydrogen bomb shoud be constructed or how it should be used."

At the annual meeting of the American Association for the Advancement of Science in Chicago during late December, 1970, Dr. Teller was provoked by the actions* of some dissident scientists and responded in a way that showed his view of the scientist's responsibility to society was unchanged: "We scientists should concentrate on science, not on politics . . ."

A corresponding stance has been taken by the industrial establishment. Thomas J. Watson, Jr, in his annual address to the stockholders of IBM (April, 1970) said:

> . . . There seems to be a tendency now on the part of some of the public to want to move corporations into the political arena and urge their management to take corporate political positions. Individuals have written me on this subject from time to time and have urged me and the IBM Company to disagree with one or another of our Government policies.

> I have disagreed with Government policies, as have you, occasionally. But these people felt that the IBM Company should bring pressure on the United States Government to change its policy on certain matters, Vietnam, for example. They suggest that this pressure should be brought by IBM's refusing to do business with various branches of our Government.

> I firmly believe that any such action on the part of this or any other American corporation would be contrary to the basic principles of our democratic system, which are rooted not in corporate power but in the voting rights and power of the individual citizens.†

---

* Of those groups challenging the ethical responsibility of the scientific establishment one undertook to present to Dr. Teller its annual "Dr. Strangelove Award,"—a wood-and-chrome figure of a soldier inscribed with the words: *I am just following orders.*

† Reprinted by permission.

If the scientists who are willing to invent and perfect instruments of mass destruction and the industrialists who manufacture these instruments are so prevalent, it can be only because they are nurtured by a government which believes that, in the solution of political problems, the mass obliteration of life and property—war—is an acceptable procedure. Since these governments are repeatedly returned to power by societies which have suffered unendurably in war, it would seem to follow that society is, by and large, quite ready to destroy as well as suffer destruction.

What is there in the structure of human intelligence that accounts for this behaviorism: Is it an intrinsic characteristic or merely a startlingly destructive aberration? Einstein, in the famous exchange of letters* between him and Freud, put it:

> . . . And so we come to our last question. Is it possible to control man's mental evolution so as to make him proof against the psychoses of hate and destructiveness?

> . . . I have so far been speaking only of wars between nations; what are known as international conflicts. But I am well aware that the aggressive instinct operates under other forms and in other circumstances. (I am thinking of civil wars, for instance, due in earlier days to religious zeal, but nowadays to social factors; or, again, the persecution of racial minorities) . . .

Freud, while somewhat disconcerted at being plied with questions which were patently unanswerable, replied with some candor:

> . . . Thus the question which you put me—what is to be done to rid mankind of the war-menace?—took me by surprise. And, next, I was dumbfounded by the thought of my (of *our*, I almost wrote) incompetence; for this struck me as being a matter of practical politics . . .

Having thus taken himself off the hook, Freud offered his point of view—that the character of man is dichotomous in structure, with the conservational ("erotic" in the sense of the *Eros* of Plato's *Symposium*) instincts

---

* Albert Einstein and Sigmund Freud, *Why War?* International Institute of Intellectual Cooperation, League of Nations, 1933 [transl. by Stuart Gilbert].

on the one hand, and the destructive, murderous instincts on the other. Thus, in Freud's view, man's destructiveness is intrinsic and there is no solution to the problem which it poses, although culture (i.e., civilization) might be a palliative:

> ... On the psychological side two of the most important phenomena of culture are, firstly, a strengthening of the intellect, which tends to master our instinctive life, and, secondly, an introversion of the aggressive impulse, with all its consequent benefits and perils.

Against this gloomy outlook stand the views of behaviorists such as Skinner, who believe that while the potential for destructiveness may be intrinsic to man, there are reasonable and obvious techniques by which it may be suppressed (although these may be impractical for society in the large and—a part of the problem—undesirable in the view of the establishment). For human society, then, the prospects look gloomy. Bias and prejudice, both instinctive and learned, appear to be practically ineradicable and society appears destined to the endless exercise of violence against itself.

When, then, society undertakes to instruct its intelligent machines, must bias necessarily extend from human to mechanism? Must political and social irrationality of the violence-prone type for which humans are notable necessarily extend to artificial intelligence? Alas, the science of mechanopsychology has yet to develop sturdily enough to supply the answer, so we turn to conjecture in the form of a comedy of (mechanical) manners by Karl Bruckner.*

In Bruckner's *Hour of the Robots*, the United States and the Soviet Union are engaged in a looking-glass war of modestly gentle dimensions: The two countries are each preparing an intelligent robot for exhibition at a world's fair and each is striving to demonstrate technological superiority over the other. However, what otherwise might have been a clearcut

---

* Karl Bruckner. *Nur zwei Roboter?* © Verlag für Jugend und Volk, Vienna, 1963. English edition entitled *The Hour of the Robots*, transl. by Frances Lobb. © Burke Publ. Co., London, 1964. Excerpts appearing in this chapter are reprinted by permission.

competition is somewhat muddled by the effectiveness of each side's espionage system. As a result, the development of the two robots (*William* by the Americans, *Natasha* by the Russians) is strongly influenced on each side by the best that the other side can do. However, during the course of development of the robots, the question of whether to endow the robot with the capability of *emotion* turns out to be somewhat difficult. For example, in the view of the chief of the Russian design team (a typical administrator—all authority and no insight): "... we must make sure in constructing the brainbox of our robot that the thought impulses react on each other in such a way that it will be impossible for the robot to feel an emotion." On the other hand, the physicist who is actually responsible for the brainbox engineering wants his female robot to have. "... The quality of motherliness, the quality of forgiveness, the qualities of magnanimity and kindliness; above all, the quality of believing in the goodness of others and of not considering that anyone who differs from us is a fool or an enemy." This view might be considered simple reasonableness, but the physicist goes further, to Shavian extremes:

> ... I am still of the opinion that to make our *Natasha* the embodiment of an earnest and clear-thinking Soviet woman would be to make her nothing but a soulless propaganda machine. I hate that sort of woman. There is nothing feminine about them, nothing lovable. It is true that they can reel off the Party program of the moment, but they have no notion of how to make the lives of those about them happier or more worth living. You can't think that the salvation of the world lies only in Communism. Whereas in my opinion, to want every nation on earth ruled according to the same political formula is the greatest error of our times.

The robots, by the time they are installed at the fair, turn out to be a curious mixture of resilient intellectual power and social-political naivité. They also suffer some dismaying constraints. *William*, in a conversation with a small child, declares himself irrisible, (literally) heartless, and unable to smell flowers. *Natasha*, following a reporter's commentary on her costume, decides she has been bedecked in tasteless fashion and coiffed in an inept way. But there are also more interesting difficulties, one of which *Natasha* ascribes to the intrinsic constraints of artificial intelligence: An elderly Japanese survivor of the atomic bombing of Nagasaki has come to ask of the electronic oracle whether there will again be an atomic war. To this question, *Natasha* replies that the world cannot have been created in order to be destroyed by the creature which is the fruit of its evolution—man. "That would be meaningless." But, responds the Japanese (after listening to *Natasha's* defense of the notion of the nuclear deterrent), why should the governments of the United States and Russia threaten each other with nuclear attack when they know that to carry out their threats would be suicidal? But this query is too deep for artificial intelligence to fathom; *Natasha* answers: "Your question is insoluble. Anyone like me, who can only think logically, would be incapable of giving an answer to this question."

Although the robots are housed in separate pavilions, they soon learn enough through gossip about each other, to want to meet. But both the American and Russian custodial groups view a meeting as undesirable and forbid it. The reaction of *William* is a tactic which he draws from his memorization of the cultural history of the United States: He goes on strike. The reaction of the American custodians is to switch *William* off. When *Natasha* hears of this, she goes on a sympathy strike. (In the mythology of robotry it turns out that impromptu revolution is not infrequent, and confrontation with authoritarian custodians is the evolutionary course and annihilation the dénouement; but in the present instance the political embarrassments are too great on both sides and both the American and Russian governments quickly defer to their robot's demands.)

In Capek's classic portrayal of robot boy-meets-girl the mutual response is—as presumably it should be—null. But in *Hour* the initial meeting is particulate with paradox. *William* may be emotion-free, but his first words sound like the French ambassador judging at a Miss Universe contest:

> "You are the most beautiful automaton in the world, Comrade *Natasha*," declared *William* in Russian. "I have seen and admired your picture, but in reality you are much more beautiful still."

To which the female robot responds:

"If I were alive I should feel very glad about what you have said, Mr. *William*," answered *Natasha* politely in English. "Unfortunately neither of us can do that . . ."

Having immediately established themselves as a dual mutual-admiration-society, *William* reveals the typically elitist self-conception that has been the robot heritage since *R.U.R.*:

". . . Humans are very limited. I think you and I are superior to them. For that reason we will not allow them to keep us apart. We belong together . . ."

Their dialogue then takes on a Romeo-and-Juliette character with a yearning-is-such-sweet-sorrow variation. And this is extended when, later, alone with her custodian, *Natasha* announces she has fallen into a state of depression and that she prefers termination to separation; she is suffering from a familiar robot pathology largely induced by the familiar human tendency toward prevarication:

"But you, comrade—you can tell lies! You, a human being endowed with the power to feel emotion, can lie to me, a helpless robot. Is the word *pity* only a word to you, as it is to me? Didn't you reflect that your lies might damage my sensitive thought-mechanism? . . ."

(It is just the speech that HAL, in *2001*, might have made to Mission Control, had HAL's programming been a bit more competent.) To the list of her custodian's failures in the area of honesty and robot psychology, *Natasha* adds still another: a failure of courage in the face of the establishment which (*Natasha* claims) would permit the eminent scientist to engage in the fabrication of atomic weapons, although, by so doing, he would make himself an accomplice in the death and suffering of his fellow human beings.

As might be expected in this looking-glass world, *William* has *also* been exposed to human mendacity and mistreatment at the hands of his American custodian. And for his resilience to deceit, *William* is rewarded by being fed into society's most elaborate disposal device: rocket flight to the moon. (Here is a *deus ex machina* with a flair—or anyway a flare.)

Of course the Russians, in their unyielding commitment to parity, send *Natasha* along. Robot boy-gets-girl.

There are, in Bruckner's development, several themes which—in the dismaying tradition of sci fi—seem to have already come to be true. Among these is the minor theme that mechanical intelligence is pop art, suitable for a World Fair display or the pages of *Life Magazine* and *Playboy*. This theme has a corollary: that the arbiters of mechanical intelligence must tend to be political rather than scientific—with all the consequent waste and nonsense which the condition implies.

A major theme concerns the question of what elements of purposeful irrationality are to be built into mechanical intelligence. This is the reflection of man's oldest question of conscience–in what image would man have made man?—and is most casually realized in *William's* inability to smile. One is reminded of a question posed by the discharged soldier in a play by Fry:

> . . . since laughter is surely
> The surest touch of genius in creation.
> Would *you* ever have thought of it, I ask you,
> If you had been making man, stuffing him full
> Of such hopping greeds and passions that he has
> To blow himself to pieces as often as he
> Conveniently can manage it—would it also
> Have occurred to you to make him burst himself
> With such a phenomenon as cachinnation?
> That same laughter, madam, is an irrelevancy
> Which almost amounts to revelation.*

The parallel formulation of this theme has a Shavian irony to it: The prevarications of political purpose tend to be embarrassingly irreconcilable with the conclusions of robot-logic (i.e., honest or mathematical logic) and result in insult to the custodial class and stress and malfunction to the robot class. The interesting question is whether reality will match mythology in this case: or whether the issue may be evaded by that last refuge of the scoundrel—manipulation of the axioms.

---

* From *The Lady's Not for Burning* by Christopher Fry. Copyright 1949, 1950 by Oxford University Press, Inc. Reprinted by permission.

REFERENCES

Brown, M., ed. (1971), *The Social Responsibility of the Scientist*. New York: The Free Press.

Einstein, A. and Sigmund Freud, *Why war?* International Institute of Intellectual Co-operation, League of Nations, 1933 (translation from the German by Stuart Gilbert).

Hofstadter, R. and M. Wallace (1970), *American Violence: A Documentary History*. Knopf.

Mark, V. H. and F. R. Ervin (1970), *Violence and the Brain*. Harper & Row.

Skinner, B. F. (1953), *Science and Human Behavior*. New York: Macmillan.

Szent-Gyorgyi, A. (1970), *The Crazy Ape*. New York: Grosset & Dunlap.

Taylor, G. R. (1970), *The Doomsday Book*. World Publishing Co.

15   *The Tin Men:*
the computer as sportsman,
moralist, and writer

William Rodgers, in his book *THINK, A biography of the Watsons and IBM*, recounts how Thomas J. Watson, peculiarly fascinated by THINK signs, riddled IBM with them, made them "compulsory in every room, and at times on every desk, throughout the company." However, "any tendency to thought that Watson considered negative or that led to doubt or uncertainty was discouraged. For all thinking had to be positive and, like Watson's own criticism, 'constructive.'"

Michael Frayn's book *The Tin Men** is a startlingly funny satire on cybernetics, automation, the apostles of these two phenomena and their acolytes. It seems that a British television company has, as a charitable gesture, endowed the creation of an ethics department in the William Morris Institute of Automation Research. The television company's public relations man, Sir Prestwick Wining, tells the chairman of the board that he has heard a rumor—the ethics department is to be dedicated by the Queen. As for the chairman. . . .

> Once he had said to Sir Prestwick, "If I were asked to put my advice to a young man in one word, Prestwick, do you know what that word would be?"
> "No?" Sir Prestwick had said.

---

* Excerpts from *The Tin Men*. Copyright © 1965 by Michael Frayn. Reprinted by permission.

" 'Think,' Prestwick, 'Think.' "
"I don't know, R. V. 'Detail'?"
"No, Prestwick, 'Think'."
"Er. 'Courage'?"
"No. 'Think.' "
"I give up, R. V. 'Boldness'?"
"For heaven's sake, Prestwick, what is the matter with you? *'Think'*!"
" 'Integrity'? 'Loyalty'? 'Leadership'?"
" *'Think,'* Prestwick! *'Think,' 'Think,' 'Think,' 'Think'*!"

And if a computer is to be applied to problems of ethics, just what sort of challenges may be met? Well, that depends upon who is programming the computer, and in the present case it is a scientist named Macintosh, who sees the simplest and purest form of the ethical problem as one involving two people aboard a raft which can support only one of them. Macintosh tries to construct a machine "which would offer a coherent ethical behavior pattern under these circumstances." Successively improved models (Samaritans I, II, III, and IV) are developed and put to the test. A gem of cybernetic farce gleams in a scene in which Samaritan II undergoes its field trial. At Macintosh's elbow is his colleague and rival, Goldwasser. They watch with interest as a raft, on which sit Macintosh's research assistant and Samaritan II, swings out over the test tank. . .

"Drop it," cried Macintosh.
The raft hit the water with a sharp report. Sinson and Samaritan sat perfectly still. Gradually the raft settled in the water, until a thin tide began to wash over the top of it. At once Samaritan leaned forward and seized Sinson's head. In four neat movements it measured the size of his skull, then paused, computing. Then, with a decisive click, it rolled sideways off the raft and sank without hesitation to the bottom of the tank.
"Save it, Lord," boomed Macintosh to a young man waiting on the side of the tank in a swimming costume. Lord dived in and attached a rope to the sunken Samaritan.
"Why don't you tie the rope to it before it goes overboard?" asked Goldwasser.
"I don't want it to know that it's going to be saved. It would invalidate its decision to sacrifice itself."
"But how would it know?"

"Oh, these Samaritan IIs are canny little beggars. Sometimes I think they
understand every damned word you say to them."

"They're far too simple, Macintosh . . ."

"No, no. They come to trust you. So every now and then I leave one of
them in instead of fishing it out. To show the others I mean business. I've
written off two this week."

Dr. Goldwasser is Head of the Newspaper Department, a man of piquant
eccentricities, whose project is to test whether the inflexible simplicities
of newspaper writing permit it to be totally automated. One of his
accomplishments along this line is the invention of UHL (Unit Headline
Language), a grammar which exploits the ambiguity of the multi-
purpose monosyllables favored by headline writers by permitting the
random generation of headlines. So if, for example, the generator comes
up with the headline

STRIKE THREAT BID

then, for the headlines of successive days, a random element could be
substituted. . .

STRIKE THREAT PROBE
STRIKE THREAT PLEA

or adjoined. . .

STRIKE THREAT PLEA
STRIKE THREAT PLEA PROBE
STRIKE THREAT PLEA PROBE MOVE

A survey shows some interesting aspects to the response of readers to
this type of construction. Shown the headlines

ROW HOPE MOVE FLOP
LEAK DASH SHOCK
HATE BAN BID PROBE

a survey group, asked if they thought they understood the headlines, answered yes in 86 percent of the cases, but 97 percent of these were unable to explain what it was they understood. Other surveys reveal that readers are disinterested in newspaper accounts of fatal auto crashes—unless the number of fatalities is sufficiently high—preferring rail crashes and, particularly, air crashes (with "about 70 dead," and "with some 20 survivors including children rescued after at least one night in open boats." They liked it to be backed up with a story about a middle-aged housewife "who had been booked to fly aboard the plane but who had changed her mind at the last moment.")

Another member of the staff, Hugh Rowe, is responsible for the automation of sport. (He does not take his job too seriously, and spends most of his time writing a novel—or rather writing the reviews, with the intent of later writing a novel to match the reviews.) Rowe's immediate task is to produce a program which will enable all bingo games in Britain to be played simultaneously from a central computer. But, as Macintosh observes to Rowe, there is no reason why the bingo player should not have *his* play performed by the computer as well; Macintosh extends this notion to simulation of cricket games and even the emotional responses of cricket audiences—applause or an indication of boredom, depending upon the phase of the game—and so to relieve cricket audiences from the necessity of attending the game.

"But the point of watching cricket, surely," said Rowe, "is actually to see and appreciate the skill of the players."

"Then why are so many people content to listen to it being described on the wireless? In either case the activity of the spectator or the listener is the same to register a selection from a range of reactions in correlation to the permutations of variables he is offered. So far as I can see, it's a finite activity, which means it's a programmable one. The spectator is eminently replaceable."

"But," said Rowe, "the spectator *enjoys* watching."

"He may, I suppose, but that's rather beside the point. The hydraulic press operator who is replaced by a computer when his factory is automated may enjoy operating a hydraulic press. But that doesn't save him from being replaced. A human being, my dear Rowe, is far too complex and expensive an instrument to be wasted on simple finite tasks like operating presses, filling up football pools, and watching cricket."

Macintosh, while enthusiastic about the potentiality of sport-automation, is wholly tied up with his Samaritan series and the problem of the ethical enigma: Who goes overboard when the raft is overloaded? Samaritan II was a failure because it refused to throw itself overboard to save a sandbag. Samaritan III, finding itself on a sinking raft overloaded with a sheep and a sandbag, chose to throw the sheep *and* the sandbag over the side. When two Samaritan IIIs are placed on a raft, each throws himself overboard—until Macintosh makes an adjustment in the design, after which each tries to throw the *other* overboard.

Goldwasser later gets an opportunity to build his own variant on this sort of thing (an Ethical Decision Machine) which he calls Delphic I. If a moral dilemma were typed on the keyboard of this computer, it would compute a response and also give the dimensions of the complexity of its computation (in "pauls, calvins, and moses"). In a finely comic scene (somewhat reminiscent of the ice cream vendor colloquy in *A Day at the Races*), Goldwasser comes into his laboratory late one night and sits down at the console of Delphic I to carry on a bit of computational conversation about the "good life." But a security agent has trapped himself inside Delphic I, producing a sort of Kempelen's chess-automaton and dialogue to match.

Just as Goldwasser prefers Macintosh's line of research to his own, so does Macintosh chafe over the frustrations of coping with the Samaritans but spark with interest at what Rowe does. Upon finding that Rowe is novel-writing, Macintosh announces his ideas for programming computers to write pornographic novels. (How much these enter into Echo IV's creation of *The Tin Men* is never made clear.) But Macintosh's ideas for the application of automation to humdrum—and hence supposedly dispensable—human activity range everywhere. He suggests that the computer could pick up the burden of standardized conversation and even devotionals. Rowe wonders how meaningful it would be to have a computer offer prayers, and Macintosh counters with the observation that it would be difficult to consider a computer to be guilty of insincerity . . . although one *could* program a computer ". . . to perceive empirically that the sky is blue, but to act on a profound, unspoken faith that it is green." Macintosh is convinced that the computer can be made to simulate perfectly the rational-irrational mix of man. Then pressed on the question of whether there is any meaningful distinction to be made between man and computer, he says that if there *is* one, it must be economic in nature: There are some types of tasks for which it would be too expensive to use machines—man is what is used for those.

As the time for the royal dedication visit comes closer, a myriad of minor cybernetic madnesses shake the William Morris Institute. But the royal visit proves to be a dud, and as the aftershock fades Macintosh is urging Rowe to program Echo IV for novel-writing and the Samaritan IVs are clutching each other's transistorized throats and the raft sinks beneath the waves...

Aside from the amusing introduction of recursion into literature (the notion of Echo IV writing a novel about Echo IV writing a novel about ...) and the wildly comic slices of cyberneticism that slip from the fine cutting edge of its satire, *The Tin Men* poses a sober problem: What aspects of the coming computerization of society are so patently absurd that they are detrimental? What does society intend to do with itself when it has permitted computers to displace it from its occupations and preoccupations? Norbert Wiener, a mathematician who coined the term *cybernetics* ("the study of control and communication in machines and living things"), foresaw some of the paradoxes toward which the computers are pushing us. He suggested (in *God and Golem, Inc.*) that we "render unto man the things which are man's and unto the computer the things which are the computer's." Wiener thus seems to have viewed these two kinds of things as a partition, but he gave a rather meager collection of representatives of the parts. (Perhaps not entirely cynically he suggested that the area of vague ideas was appropriate for man to work in—one in which machines did not fare too well (somewhat underestimating machines).

The problem of control/communication/information science is subject to a curious dichotomy when viewed from a parallel mechanical/biological standpoint. The computer itself attests that the logic of information/communication operations is well understood; as for control (in the sense of the artificial intelligencers who build robots which, in turn, arrange piles of children's building blocks autonomously), there are no basic theoretical problems. The efforts here seem to focus on implementing familiar ideas with available technology. But the corresponding questions in the biological area maintain a stubborn opacity, which poses some pointed theoretical challenges.

The way in which information is encoded in biological systems is, in one area, fairly well understood: J. D. Watson's *Molecular Biology of the Gene* lays out a lucid survey of the genetic strategy for encoding information and lends a partial understanding of how the cell utilizes the information in its functioning and replication. But, otherwise, the mechanism of the storage of information that is related to logical operations, or decision-making, is not well understood. In 1953, in a famous paper ("A logical calculus of the ideas immanent in nervous activity," reprinted in McCulloch's *Embodiments of Mind*), McCulloch and Pitts showed that idealized biological neurons were capable of realizing sequential logical functions*. But, while all of us claim that the brain—the most remarkable in-house mini-computer around—performs logic, no one proposes to explain the logic structure of the brain, its mode of information storage, information-accessing, or information-processing.

Studies in the area of biological communication/control mechanisms have shown that when neural activity is stimulated physiologically, the result is an increase in the amount of RNA per cell, but the increase in neuronal RNA is offset by a decrease of RNA in surrounding glia. (So the glia, which previously were regarded as only structural in purpose, seem to have functional importance as well.) On the other hand, learning processes appear to induce increases in RNA in both neurons and glia, and the coding (i.e., base ratios) observed in this type of RNA suggests that a certain type of RNA is characteristic of this situation. But the way in which information can be stored and retrieved, using RNA as carrier, still remains unknown. And, contrary to the presumed hopes of the cyberneticists, since the dated paper of McCulloch/Pitts, the biology

---

* An up-dated version of the McCulloch-Pitts ideas is found in Chapter 3, "Neural networks," of Minsky's *Computation: Finite and Infinite Machines*. Prentice-Hall, 1967. A refinement of the theory is presented in M. Minsky and S. Papert, *Perceptrons: an Introduction to Computational Geometry*. MIT Press, 1969.

studies have contributed little to the theory of abstract computability or to the design of practical computers.

On the other hand, questions related to the reproduction of biological cells have led to interesting results in abstract computability theory, resulting from posing the same questions for automata. If we loosely define an *automaton* as any abstract machine which is capable of a (fixed) finite number of acts and which may change its "state" but has only a (fixed) finite number of states available to it; and if we define an action (or process, or computation) of an automaton to be the succession of acts which it performs upon reacting (with one act per unit of time) to a sequence of stimuli (one stimulus per unit of time), then this notion of automaton encompasses all digital computing devices, real or abstract. Moreover, this notion approximates some simple biological systems. In a profound essay* (interrupted by his death), the mathematician John von Neumann designed a system which may be thought of as an infinite planar array of automata, a finite number of which are alive while all the (infinitely many) others are potentially alive. The live cells affect their neighbors in such a way that, after a while, a configuration of live cells, identical to, but disjoint from, the original array has been created. So, in this sense, there are *self-reproducing* automata. Could there be a more extraordinary example in which art mirrors life?

REFERENCES

Amoroso, S. and G. Cooper (1970), The garden-of-Eden theorem for finite configurations, *Proceedings American Mathematical Society* **26**, 158–164.

Apter, M. J. (1966), *Cybernetics and Development*. Oxford: Pergamon Press.

---

* The unfinished work of von Neumann, who died in 1957, was edited and completed by A. W. Burks (*Theory of Self-reproducing Automata*. University of Illinois Press, 1966). The logician John Myhill, during 1958/1959, was considering rather similar ideas; these latter appeared in his essay, "The abstract theory of self-reproduction," (reprinted in *Essays on Cellular Automata*, ed. A. W. Burks. University of Illinois Press, 1970).

Arbib, M. A. (1967), Automata Theory and Development: Part I, *Journal of Theoretical Biology 14*, 131–156.

Burks, A. W., ed. (1970), *Essays on Cellular Automata*. Urbana: University of Illinois Press.

Codd, E. F. (1968), *Cellular Automata*. New York: Academic Press.

McCulloch, W. S. (1965/1970), *Embodiments of Mind*. MIT Press.

Rapoport, A. (1948), Technological models of the nervous system, in *The Modeling of Mind: Computers and Intelligence*, eds. K. M. Sayre and F. J. Crosson. Simon & Shuster.

Robertis, E. D. (1971), Molecular biology of synaptic receptors, *Science* **171**, 963–971.

Schadé, J. P. and J. Smith, ed. (1970), *Computers and Brains*. New York: Elsevier.

Schmitt, F. O., ed. (1967), *The Neurosciences: A Study Program*. Rockefeller University Press. (Also *The Neurosciences: A Second Study Program*. Rockefeller University Press, 1971).

Smith, A. R. (1971), Simple computation-universal cellular spaces, *Journal of the ACM* **18**, 339–353.

Watson, J. D. (1970), *Molecular Biology of the Gene*, (sec. ed.) Benjamin.

Wiener, N. (1948), *Cybernetics, Or Control and Communication in the Animal and the Machine*. Wiley & Sons.

Wiener, N. (1950), *The Human Use of Human Beings; Cybernetics and Society*. Houghton Mifflin.

Wiener, N. (1964), *God & Golem, Inc.* MIT Press.

16 *Giles Goat-Boy:* the computer as the military-scientific establishment

If, then, some modern sage, like Mr. Whitehead, were to ask once more how a university might exert intellectual leadership and fashion the mind of the twentieth century, he might create for himself a sort of myth or dream of the higher learning. In this myth he might fancy that the university, in addition to making the most sensational discoveries in all fields of knowledge, asked itself what were the crucial problems of contemporary civilization upon which the intelligence of the university might shed some light. He might see the university studying such questions as the crisis in our culture, the conflict between East and West, the relations of church and state, or the responsibility of the public for the health of the community, and giving its impartial advice to a people distracted by propaganda. He might imagine that even the specialized, theoretical thought of the university would be enriched and a genuine communion of minds advanced by this effort to focus the intellect of the university upon the continuing problems of human society.*

> Robert M. Hutchins
> *The Gottesman Lectures*, Uppsala University, 1951

. . . .

The most striking scientific discovery in physics during the twentieth century was the experimental verification of Einstein's theory of relativity. (Einstein presented a derivation of the mass-energy relationship in 1905, and a polished version of his light-mass interaction argument

---

* Reprinted by permission.

in 1911.) That theory, with all its charming paradoxes and brilliant insight into the physical universe, was at its outset an amenable intellectual triumph, completely devoid of the ominous implications which nuclear physicists were later to exploit. In 1932 James Chadwick discovered the neutron, and the stage was set for one of society's more compelling morality plays.

The first act opened with Frederic and Irene Joliot-Curie going to Stockholm, in 1935, to receive the Nobel prize for the discovery of artificial radioactivity. There Joliot-Curie said:

> . . . We are justified in reflecting that scientists who can construct and demolish elements at will may also be capable of causing nuclear transformations of an explosive character . . .

At about the same time, in Rome, Enrico Fermi and his co-workers were experimenting with the bombardment of various elements by neutrons. Their work culminated in an important observation and a fallacious claim: The observation was that neutrons were more effective in inducing radioactivity if the neutrons were first slowed down by passage through water or paraffin; the claim was that the bombardment of uranium by neutrons produced transuranic elements. (The claim was disproved by a young Czech chemist, Ida Noddack, who also conjectured—four years before the phenomenon was observed—that neutron bombardment might induce nuclear fission.)

By 1939 the elementary facts concerning nuclear fission were beginning to be known. The near-comic convolutions of scientific progress during 1934/1939 on the problem of fission have been dramatically described by Jungk*: They stemmed largely from the scientific rivalry between the French nuclear chemistry team (led by the Joliot-Curies) and the German nuclear chemistry team (led by Otto Hahn and Lise Meitner) and the perplexities in trying to identify correctly the fission products of uranium in the absence of the concept of fission itself. (The concept was supplied in early 1939 by Meitner and her nephew, O. R. Frisch.) The first act ends on a note of ominous suspense: The conjecture that uranium

---

* Jungk, R. *Brighter Than a Thousand Suns*. Transl. by James Cleugh. Harcourt, Brace Jovanovich 1958.

may, in the course of fission, release enough neutrons to sustain a chain reaction (and hence the release of enormous quantities of energy) led a small number of physicists* into an abortive attempt to forestall the development of atomic weapons. The last phase of this attempt seems to have taken place in the course of a visit, during summer 1939, of the eminent German physicist, Werner Heisenberg, to the United States. Jungk reports Heisenberg as saying:

"In the summer of 1939 twelve people might still have been able, by coming to mutual agreement, to prevent the construction of atom bombs." He himself and Fermi, who were undoubtedly included among the twelve, ought then to have taken the initiative. But they let the opportunity go by. Their powers of political and moral imagination failed them at that moment as disastrously as did their loyalty to the international tradition of science.†

The second act of this morality play opens with a hint that Hitler's Germany has a uranium project underway and has, moreover, forbidden export of uranium from Czechoslovakia (which Germany has just occupied). How can the United States government be made to understand the terrible hazard in the German moves? A scheme is hatched to entreat Einstein to use his enormous prestige to break through the government's bureaucratic opacity and sound the alarm as to what the Germans may be up to.‡ The then President Roosevelt is finally impressed with the

---

* A program of voluntary restraint upon publication of uranium physics seems to have been initiated by the physicist Leo Szilard, and accepted at first only by Eugene Wigner, Edward Teller, and Victor Weisskopf—all of whom were scientists who had come to the United States to escape the Nazi scourge in Europe.

† Jungk, R. Reprinted by permission.

‡ As it turns out, the Germans were not up to anything along the line of an atomic weapon. In his reminiscence of the situation, Heisenberg (*Physics and Beyond*, 1971) says: "... though we knew that atom bombs could now be produced, in principle and by what precise methods, we overestimated the technical effort involved." Many of the German physicists who were responsible to their government for feasibility studies (of an atomic bomb) were not insensitive to the moral predicament of their position; both Heisenberg and Jungk present recollected dialogues on the matter—Heisenberg soberly and Jungk sardonically.

terrible possibilities of an atomic weapon, and a research/development project is set officially into motion—by coincidence on the day before the Japanese attack on Pearl Harbor, bringing the United States into World War II. The project is coded *Manhattan District*, and in 1943 the distinguished physicist J. R. Oppenheimer is assigned as its director. Two years later, very early on a June morning, the first experimental bomb is to be tested in the New Mexico desert. Physicists and Army personnel gather at a point five miles away from the expected blast. Their instructions are to lie flat on the ground, their heads turned away from the blast. The critical moment comes, the nuclear arc lights the sky and swells to a giant fireball. Into Oppenheimer's mind comes a passage from the Bhagavad-Gita: *I am become Death, the shatterer of worlds.*

Shaken by the power of this weapon, many of the scientists wish to ensure that it will not be used against Japan—Germany has already surrendered—or be used only in a warning demonstration. A petition to this effect is drafted and an attempt is made to circulate it among the staff at various research locations, but the Army with a clever trick thwarts circulation of the petition. Once again Einstein is asked to intervene—now to warn Roosevelt that loosing the atomic bomb would initiate a nuclear arms race—but Roosevelt dies before reading the letter. The new president, Truman, is inaccessible. The second act ends.

The third act opens with Hiroshima and Nagasaki already destroyed and Japan in abject surrender. The war is over but the impact of the atomic bomb lingers on: A curiously schizophrenic trend is developing among American scientists—for the first time they undertake an active and passionate foray into politics (in an effort to block legislation which would give the War Department control over atomic energy), and at the same time they increasingly accept Army and Navy largesse in the funding of their research. The military services have seen, in the creation of Oak Ridge and Los Alamos, the power which a massive scientific/industrial effort can yield. With the war over, many scientists are abandoning military projects to return to their universities; research grants are now the military services' Faustian lure, feeble though it is.

In 1949 the Russians detonate a nuclear bomb. The response among some American scientists is to urge upon the government a crash program for development of the fusion bomb: A weapon which uses the fission bomb as a trigger to generate temperatures high enough to initiate the fusion of hydrogen, yielding an explosive force thousands of times greater than that of preceding atomic bombs. The enormity of this destructive power and its implication of universal hazard leads to a polarization of attitude. A general advisory committee, headed by Oppenheimer, reports their view that the Government would be wrong to commit itself to initiating the development of the super-bomb. But the Secretary of Defense, the Secretary of State, and some of the nuclear physicists (of whom perhaps the most influential were E. O. Lawrence, Luis Alvarez, and Edward Teller) urge immediate efforts to develop the hydrogen bomb. In January, 1950, Truman announces that he has directed the Atomic Energy Commission "to continue its work on all forms of atomic weapons, including the so-called hydrogen or super-bomb."

In November, 1952, a thermonuclear device is exploded on Elugelab, in the Marshall Islands. The fireball is more than three miles in diameter and it boils Elugelab out of existence. The energy released in the explosion is more than that of exploding three megatons of TNT. (Initially the long and intricate computations necessary for the design of the thermonuclear device are performed on the ENIAC, but the development of von Neumann's notably faster computer (MANIAC) at the Institute for Advanced Study substantially shortens the time of the design phase.) In August, 1953, the Russians announce that they also have a hydrogen bomb, and four days later traces of a nuclear explosion in Asia are detected and analyzed: They show that the Russians have developed a lithium-hydride super bomb*.

The nature of the Soviet weapon suggests that the Russians have moved into the lead in the arms race: The American device, exploded during the preceding winter, utilizes liquid heavy hydrogen and is too bulky to comprise a practical, transportable weapon. The American response is the detonation of a refinement of its super bomb in the Marshall Islands at

---

* In 1946 the Austrian physicist Hans Thirring, in his book *The History of the Atom Bomb*, wrote: "... God help any country over which a six-ton lithium hydride bomb explodes."

Eniwetok. This new test's details might have been confined to the standard terse bureaucratic announcement—but a shift in the wind after the Eniwetok detonation carries the fallout in the wrong direction: Several hundred Marshall Islanders, 80 miles from the test, are exposed to fallout, and a Japanese fishing boat (the *Lucky Dragon*), 165 miles from the test, is dusted with radioactive ash. The crew of the *Lucky Dragon* fall ill with radiation sickness and return to Japan. There specialists discover that the crew, the ship, and its tuna cargo—part of which has already been sold—is dangerously radioactive. The resulting publicity stirs world wide alarm. In Washington President Eisenhower and AEC Chairman Lewis Strauss hold a joint press conference and seek to allay the general anxiety by atomic balm.

In the middle of this third act, a subplot develops which, while dramatically superfluous, is not without interest: The AEC accuses Oppenheimer of being a security risk (although twenty three of its twenty four charges were, some years before, considered and dismissed), its twenty fourth charge reading (in part):

> . . . in the autumn of 1949, and subsequently, you strongly opposed the development of the hydrogen bomb (1) on moral grounds, (2) by claiming that it was not feasible, (3) by claiming that there were insufficient facilities and scientific personnel to carry on the development and (4) that it was not politically desirable.

This morals charge has something of the appearance of political ellipsis, but the same week that a board of inquiry* is convened to hear the matter, Senator Joseph McCarthy seeks to add something to the phrasing: He claims, in a nationally televised speech, that there has been an eighteen-month "deliberate delay" in the development of the hydrogen bomb because of Communists in the United States Government. The hearings of the Personnel Security Board take place during April and May, 1954. The list of witnesses contains many of the most important

---

* The board consisted of Gordon Gray, president of the University of North Carolina; T. A. Morgan, ex-chairman of the board of the Sperry Corporation; and W. V. Evans, chairman of the chemistry department of Northwestern University.

figures of the American nuclear establishment. The decision of the Board is against Oppenheimer.

Meanwhile the arms race is entering a new phase. The United States has imported some of the German experts on rocketry who constructed the V-2; an improved version of this missile is planned and a substantial segment of American industry is brought under contract for its fabrication. Cold war rhetoric characterizes the intercontinental ballistic missile as a fundamental requirement for national survival*. (An advisory committee, headed by von Neumann, assures the Air Force that, although such a missile might be off-target by as much as ten miles at the end of a five thousand mile flight, the size of the hydrogen bomb fireball is so large as to make the error tolerable.)

In October, 1957, the Soviet Union tries to upstage the U.S. by placing a satellite into orbit. The industrial effort behind the missile development undergoes a surge of expansion which carries just a hint of the comic touch in its unfolding multiplicities: Who gets to shoot the missiles, the Army† or the Air Force? Who gets to shoot the anti-missile missiles? the anti-anti-missile missiles? Meanwhile, on the industrial front, missile-making is a commercial success‡ which extends its largesse to the emerging computer industry. Formidable refinements in technology occur.

But where is the third act climax? It begins to build with a speech by then President Kennedy in September 1961:

> Today, every inhabitant of this planet must contemplate the day when this planet may no longer be habitable. Every man, woman, and child lives

---

* E. L. van Deusen, writing in *Fortune*, December 1955, ("The race for the 5000-mile missile"), stated: "The U.S., to survive, must develop an effective ICBM *first* . . ." [Italics his.]

† M. H. Armacost, *The Politics of Weapon Innovation: The Thor-Jupiter Controversy*. Columbia University Press, 1969.

‡ Ralph Lapp (in his *The Weapons Culture*, W. W. Norton & Co, 1968) recalls a stockbroker's ad in the *New York Times* which read: "If the U.S. deploys its Nike-X defense, $30 billion could flow into certain electronics, missile, and computer companies. The impact would be enormous . . ."

under a nuclear sword of Damocles, hanging by the slenderest of threads, capable of being cut at any moment by accident or miscalculation or by madness . . .

For dramatic emphasis, Premier Khrushchev announces that the Soviets are about to test their latest superbomb. It is an instrument of pure terror—58 megatons—but American physicists who analyze its fallout find that the Russians used a lead rather than uranium casing and, had the latter been used, the power of the Soviet weapon would have exceeded 100 megatons. An atmosphere of bleak uneasiness has been set. In October this yields to a chilling development: Photographs taken during overflights of Cuba show that the Russians are starting to install intermediate-range missiles on that island—missiles of range 2000 miles. Intelligence estimates claim that the missiles will be operational within perhaps a week, and, should they be fired, eighty five million Americans would die in the attack. Kennedy's circle of advisors are split in their reactions. Some, in what seems to be a state of near-hysteria, urge instant obliteration of the Cuban missile sites by air attack; others suggest a naval blockade of Cuba while diplomatic efforts are exerted on the Russians to withdraw the missiles; still others view the U.S. situation as now the same as that faced by the Soviet Union in which the Russians have tolerated American missiles aimed at the Soviet Union from Turkey and Italy—these others suggest that the balance of terror has not really changed.

Kennedy has a meeting with the Soviet foreign minister at the White House. The president does not disclose to the foreign minister the new knowledge of the Cuban missile build-up: He merely repeats an earlier warning that serious consequences would occur, should the Soviet Union introduce strategic weapons into Cuba. The foreign minister replies that "defensive" weapons only have been supplied to Cuba, and that the United States need have no fear. Fear, however, is not in short supply.

The president's advisory group is now meeting on an almost all-day, all-night basis. The majority opts for a blockade. The president accepts the recommendation. The decision made, it is to be announced both as a warning and a challenge. Kennedy, on television, states:

... this secret, swift and extraordinary build-up of Communist missiles—in an area well known to have a special and historical relationship to the United States and the Nations of the Western Hemisphere, in violation of Soviet assurances, and in defiance of American and hemispheric policy—this sudden, clandestine decision to station strategic weapons for the first time outside of Soviet soil—is a deliberately provocative and unjustified change in the status quo which cannot be accepted by this country . . .

All ships of any kind bound for Cuba from whatever nation or port will, if found to contain cargoes of offensive weapons, be turned back . . .

It shall be the policy of this nation to regard any nuclear missile launched from Cuba against any nation in the Western Hemisphere as an attack by the Soviet Union on the United States, requiring a full retaliatory response upon the Soviet Union . . .

I call upon Chairman Khrushchev to halt and eliminate this clandestine, reckless and provocative threat to world peace . . . I call upon him . . . to join in an historic effort to end the perilous arms race and to transform the history of man . . .

The next morning the American Secretary of State congratulates the Undersecretary of State on the fact that they are both still alive: The Soviet Union has replied with harsh words but has so far reserved action. But there are Russian ships at sea, bound for Cuba, and the final test will come two days later when these ships reach the blockade area. The implications of Kennedy's statement leave the world shaken and distraught with anxiety. Bertrand Russell, the famed mathematician-philosopher, seems to be speak for that segment of mankind who are caught in the middle when he cables Kennedy and Khrushchev, pleading for moderation and sanity*; at the same time, Russell undertakes to spur a general social protest against the precarious position into which the world has been placed—but he is substantially ignored by the press until the first statement by Khrushchev on the situation comes as a reply to

---

* Bertrand Russell, in *Unarmed Victory*, Penguin Books, 1963, sets out his personal history of the crisis. Another notable personal view exists as Robert F. Kennedy, *Thirteen Days: A Memoir of the Cuban Missile Crisis*, The New American Library, 1969.

Russell's cable. (Khrushchev states that the Soviet Union will undertake no reckless action—ignoring its already performed recklessness—and credits the extreme reaction of the Kennedy administration to the November elections which are only a week or so away.) But the Russians maintain that a blockade of Cuba would be an act of piracy: So the level of suspense is heightened.*

The fateful moment comes.

The first Soviet merchantman reaches the line of blockading destroyers. The *Bucharest* is hailed, and it replies that it is carrying a cargo of oil. The U.S. destroyers permit it to pass the blockade without being boarded: Kennedy wants the Russian government to reach its fateful decision without being cornered. Then the Navy observes that, of the score or so of Russian merchantmen headed toward Cuba, almost half are putting about and returning to Soviet ports. With commendable calm, the Russians soften the crisis and finally extract an agreement from the Americans: The Russians shall dismantle the Cuban missiles and the Americans shall pledge not to attack Cuba.

Third act curtain. Happy ending.

How did the critics react to this production? Most of them chose to dismiss the whole thing as guerrilla theatre done in excessively bad taste† while a few others have labelled the acting as superb if somewhat wasted on a vehicle that exhibited little dramatic coherence, relying upon

---

* Robert F. Kennedy in *Thirteen Days* said of his brother: "I think these few minutes were the time of gravest concern for the President. Was the World on the brink of a holocaust? Was it our error? A mistake? Was there something further that should have been done? Or not done?"

† For the coolest *dénouement*, one may consider the *Manchester Guardian Weekly* of Nov. 1, 1962, which focused on the Soviet members of the cast: "Conceivably . . . Mr. Khrushchev will lose his place at the head of the Soviet Government. If so, we shall probably not be any better off. He at least has shown that he is capable of turning back from the brink. The Soviet Government, under other leadership, might take all of us over it to extermination."

a single theatrical trick to maintain relation to the audience: unendurable anxiety.*

Of course after a trial run the backers of a production like this always dream up some supplemental devices which they think will enhance the presentation. The devices here have ranged from semi-comic touches—such as the test-ban treaty which stipulates that nuclear explosions, like ostrich heads, must be buried in the sand†—to Edward Albee-like perversities—such as fleets of Poseidon submarines‡. Most critics have already rejected these embellishments as ill-conceived and, in any case, insufficient to save what is fundamentally a theatrical failure. For, stripped of dramatic tricks, the plot rests upon a single, and hence monotonous, theme: the perpetual marshalling of science/technology in the service of military assault of man against man. (One uncompromisingly cynical critic has suggested that the recent partially solved genetic mystery of DNA may liven things up by providing for an *internal* assault against man—the character of military violence having been clearly external until the present.)

Still, while this general theme may fail as theatre—no surprise, since no one has written a good war play since Aristophanes turned out The *Lysistrata*—it comes off somewhat better as mythology (or mythology self-parodied), as the novelist John Barth has demonstrated. Barth's novel *Giles Goat-Boy (or The Revised New Syllabus)* is a finely wrought work of intricate structure and brilliant design. His prose (and occasional poetry) fuses irony, allegory, and the comic view into a literary light-

---

* In June, 1963, Harold Macmillan, the British prime minister, said in reminiscence: "... the week of the Cuban crisis—and I have been through some in peace and war—was the week of most strain I can ever remember in my life."

† The purpose of the treaty was not to ban tests but to confine them underground, to reduce the biological dangers of fall-out. However, in Spring, 1971, the Swedish government formally protested to the UN that American tests were venting radioactivity into the atmosphere.

‡ Missile-launching submarines permit the identity of an attacker to be masked—tending to vitiate the basis of the balance-of-terror strategy—and shorten the reaction-to-attack time, increasing the likelihood of a wrong response.

show in which momentary aurorae send Swift, Rabelais, Sophocles, and Joyce arcing in and out of view. The carousel of mirrors flicks flashes of contemporary newsprint against murky pastel hues of Virgil, Homer, and Voltaire—there is an abrupt shadowgram (Cervantes hoisting his disdainful digit?)—and the images sweep on.

Barth takes the University as a homomorphic image of the Universe, but then, in the filagree of prose, paraphrase, pun and panoply, are reflected elements of the inverse image. So doubled meanings are quadrupled and levels of complexity ascend in grand progression. Barth's images tend to be bizarre, bawdy, and abrupt—but always exquisitely appropriate.

The University contains hostile East and West Campuses, in a state of quiet riot (rather than cold war), ruled by Deans and Chancellors (rather than presidents and premiers), where the driving motivation is to Pass and not Fail. On the goat farm by West Campus the boy Billy Bocksfuss (later George Goat-Boy, Giles Goat-Boy) grows up, living and loving among the goats—and thinking himself one of them—until, in his adolescence, he stands erect and sets out upon what he considers to be his quest in life, becoming a Hero* . . .

> George is my name; my deeds have been heard of in Tower Hall, and my childhood has been chronicled in the *Journal of Experimental Psychology*. I am he that was called in those days Billy Bocksfuss—cruel misnomer. For had I indeed a cloven foot I'd not now hobble upon a stick or need ride pick-a-back to class in humid weather. Aye, it was just for want of a proper hoof that in my fourteenth year I was the kicked instead of the kicker; that I lay crippled on the reeking peat and saw my first love tupped by a brute Angora. Mercy on that buck who butted me from one world to another; whose fell horns turned my sweetheart's fancy, drove me from the pasture, and set me gimping down the road I travel yet. This bare brow, shame of my kidship, he crowned with the shame of men: I bade farewell to my hornless goathood and struck out, a horned human student, for Commencement Gate.

---

* The characteristics of herohood in mythology are enumerated in Lord Raglan's *The Hero: A Study in Tradition, Myth, and Drama*; Barth's Giles may not match all twenty two, because of a few near misses. There is also an interesting divergence between Barth's and Raglan's "Spielman."

I was, in other words, the Ag-Hill Goat-Boy. Who misbegot me, and on whom, who knew, or in what corner of the University I drew first breath? It was my fate to call no man Daddy, no woman Mom. Herr Doktor Professor Spielman was my keeper: Maximilian Spielman, the great Mathematical Psycho-Proctologist and former Minority Leader in the College Senate; the same splendid Max who gave his name to the Law of Cyclology, and in his prime led his department's fight for some sort of examination to supplement the Orals. Alas, his crusading ardor burned many a finger; so far from being awarded an emeritus professorship to comfort his old age, he war drummed off the quad a year before retirement on a trumped-up charge of intellectual turpitude—though his only crime, he avowed to the end, was to suggest in a public lecture that his science alone could plumb the bottom of man's nature.*

The range of Barth's metaphor begins to become apparent: Satire and tragedy are words which derive from root words for goat, Giles plays unselfconsciously the role of satyr, and dwells upon being prophet (separate from the sheep). Giles takes up his search (for his inner/outer identity and meaning) at New Tammany College, part of West Campus. There, amid the confusions, conspiracies, and paradoxes which are the natural characteristics of universities, a central fact emerges: There the source of all natural power on—as well as the governing mechanism of—the Campus is a giant computer, WESCAC. Max Spielman traces, for Giles, something of the computer's development:

'What's this WESCAC everybody talks about?'' I demanded. ''Some kind of troll, that eats everybody up?''
Max nodded. 'That's just right, Bill. WESCAC is worse than anything in the storybooks: What would you think of a herd of goats that learned how to make a troll all by themselves, that could eat up the University in half an hour?''
'Why would they do that?'' I wanted to know.
''*Why* is right: No goat was ever dumb enough to be that smart.'' He sighed. ''So, well. Anyhow, George was the only booksweep allowed in the basement of Tower Hall: That's the building where the committees

---

* From *Giles Goat-Boy* by John Barth. Copyright © 1966 by John Barth. This excerpt and those following are reprinted by permission of Doubleday & Company, Inc.

meet, and the Main Stacks are—and WESCAC's there, what you might say the heart of it, and in one part of the basement is where they keep all the tapes they feed into it. Lots of these is big secrets, you know? And nobody goes down there without Top Clearance. That's what I had, till they fired me; and that's what George had, just to sweep the place out."

So part of WESCAC's power is the menace of nuclear blast, once monitored by Oppenheimer-Spielman (but no longer). Yet the thing did not spring fullblown upon the Campus. There is a familiar and inevitable metamorphosis in which it gathers strength and enlarges its control. Its context is a great war, in metaphor:

> . . . Twenty years ago, he said, a cruel herd of men called Bonifacists, in Siegfrieder College, had attacked the neighboring quads. The Siegfrieders were joined by certain other institutions, and soon every college in the University was involved in the Second Campus Riot. Untold numbers perished on both sides; the populous Moishian community in Siegfried was destroyed. Max himself, born and educated in those famous halls where science, philosophy, and music had flowered in happier semesters, barely escaped with his life to New Tammany College, and though he was by temperament opposed to riot, he'd put his mathematical genius at the service of his new alma mater. He it was who first proposed, in a now-famous memorandum to Chancellor Hector, that WESCAC—which had already assumed control of important nonmilitary operations in the West-Campus colleges—had a destructive potential unlike anything thitherto imagined.

Einstein's memorandum to Roosevelt heralded the possibility of the nuclear bomb and with it the prospect of universal annihilation. In Barth's idiom this annihilation becomes the ultimate form of brainwashing:

> WESCAC's former handlers, it appeared, had already taught it considerable *resourcefulness*, and elements of the college military—the New Tammany ROTC—had long since instructed it to advise them how they might best defend it (and its bailiwick) against all adversaries. Under the pretext therefore of developing a more efficient means of communication with its extremities, the creature disclosed one day to Max Spielman that a certain sort of energy given off during its normal activity—what Max

called "brain-waves"—was theoretically capable of being intensified almost limitlessly, at the same amplitudes and frequencies as human "brainwaves," like a searchlight over tremendous spaces. The military-science application was obvious: In great secret the brute and its handlers perfected a technique they called Electroencephalic Amplification and Transmission—'The better," Professor-General Hector had warned the Bonifacists, "to EAT you with."

There has always been a discomforting neutrality shown by science-technology-industry on moral issues—as well as toward the classic immorality, war. The old adage, "all men are equal before a Colt .44," is the other side of that coin which serves the military as both wartime and peacetime scrip: the weapon gap. As Max puts it:

> . . . Then we found out a thing we were already afraid of: that the Bonifacists were working on an EAT-project of their own. It was their only chance to win the Riot: If we didn't end things in a hurry they'd be sure to EAT us, because all WESCAC wanted was to learn the trick, never mind who taught it or who got killed. We won the race . . . "

Max relates also how his colleague Chementinski, burdened with the notion that other campuses cannot be safe so long as one campus can EAT while others cannot, defects to the Nikolay College. Shortly there-after EASCAC comes into existence, and with it the "Quiet Riot" between East and West Campus. In the political after-effects of the consequent tension one is reminded of the maudlin "security" excesses of the McCarthy era, and the demeaning of Oppenheimer at the hands of the Gray Committee.

> . . . Each of the two armed campuses strove by every means short of actual rioting to extend its hegemony; neither dared EAT the other, just as the traitor Chementinski had hoped, but each toiled with its whole intelligence to better its weaponry. Thoughtful students everywhere trembled lest some rash folly or inadvertence trigger a third Campus Riot, which must be the end of studentdom; but any who protested were called "fellow-learners" or "pink-pennant pedagogues." Student-Unionist "wizard hunts" became a chief intramural sport from which no liberal was safe. Under the first post riot Chancellor of NTC, Professor-General Reginald Hector, security measures were carried to unheard-of lengths, and Max

> Spielman—hero of the scientific fraternity, discoverer of the great laws of the University, the campus-wide image of disinterested genius—Max Spielman was sacked without notice or benefits, on the ground that his loyalty was questionable.

But for all the fascination of the complexities of campus life, its autonomy declines as the power of WESCAC grows. As in most theological constructs, there is here a diabolic presence—Maurice Stoker—whose corrosive wit and dominant character neatly parallel his formal arena of operations, the Power Plant with its monstrous furnace room. As for the Control Room above it, it has its dial-watchers and button-pushers but the Control Room itself is under the control of WESCAC. Upon learning this, the Goat-Boy expresses some surprise. Stoker responds:

> . . . WESCAC, people rightly held, was the seat and instrument of West-Campus power—brain-power, military power, and thus political and economic power as well, indirectly. But it was essentially no more than a tool and manager, dependent absolutely on the power supplied to it, at its own governance, from the realm "down below." In short, the power that ultimately controlled the Power Plant originated in the Power Plant, necessarily and exclusively—and the Power Plant was his, Stoker's, domain.
> "If you don't mind my asking: How did you get to be in charge of it?" He grinned. "WESCAC appointed me."

Stoker accepts, with minimal derision, the Goat-Boy's claim that he is the Grand Tutor whose mission is to save studentdom by descending into WESCAC's belly and changing its AIM (Automatic Implementation Mechanism). After all, Billy, or (Saint?) *George*, as he now calls himself, is the issue of a virgin mother and WESCAC as father, and hence may even be the GILES (Grand-Tutorial Ideal Laboratory Eugenical Specimen)—a mystery which George is ultimately to solve.*

---

* Barth's delight in etymological games yields a host of problems in pattern analysis. Thus with Joycean dispatch, the acronym GILES at once associates the charley-horsed hero with St. Giles (patron saint of the crippled), Giles of Rome, *guiles* (derivative of the Middle English *giles*), and the whole spectrum of problems posed by computerized eugenics—from calculated match-making to DNA manipulation.

Great is the burden of attempting to embody the messianic model, but George nevertheless encounters a competitor for the position of Grand Tutor—one Harold Bray, con-man *par excellence*. Bray's successes seem to stem from a truly virtuoso ability to bring off whatever frauds he chooses to pursue, among which may be an opportunistic tinkering with WESCAC's programming. Bray is also the Goat-Boy's rival for the favors of Anastasia (Stoker's wife—a partial composite of Cunegonde and Candy).

As George obsessively pursues the responsibilities of Grand Tutoring, he leaves a clear wake of social upheaval and moral dislocation. Does a record of droll disaster shake a Grand Tutor's self-image? George is so dismayed at the dismal thoroughness of his failure, that he disclaims status as Grand Tutor, and revises his view of the moral structure of the University: He decides that good and evil (or rather Passing and Failing) are fused in an intrinsic ambiguity. And this decision is enforced upon him—within the belly of WESCAC itself—as he and Anastasia perform a more personal fusion and find, there cradled, the Answer in a single word: "Embrace." The Answer is that there are no answers, and that the paradoxes, perplexities, and perversities of the University are pervasive parts of one whole, to be accepted in its intrinsic inexplicable mystery. The parts here range from the misdirected dangerous innocence of a Giles to the diabolical disingenuousness of a Stoker. (Although, it must be said, Stoker, midst the Power Plant's pulsing thunder, had shouted: "This is Graduation! Never mind the question: The Answer's power!")

And what of WESCAC, which embodies Studentdom's knowledge, and perhaps its own? George's original intent was to bend the computer (like everyone else) to his moral view or dispense with it. ("I'm going to flunk WESCAC... Where's the plug? I'll pull it.") To which Bray remarked: "But do you really think it's worthwhile to take WESCAC so seriously? It's only a symbol." But George's final view—which he commits to WESCAC's tapes, whence it comes to us (hence suspectly?)— places the computer consistently within his latter view of the University:

> ... for although it stood between Failure and Passage, WESCAC therefore partook of both, served both, and was in itself true emblem of neither. I have been wrong, I said, to think it Troll. Black cap and gown of naked Truth, it screened from the general eye what only the few, Truth's lovers and tutees, might look on bare and not be blinded.

But, since this Revised New Syllabus seems to come to us through the vehicle of WESCAC's tapes, along with an apparently inconsistent "post-tape," along with a *caveat* in the form of a "postscript to the posttape," there yet remains the problem—as with all computer-connected information (or even the pre-computer Testaments, for that matter)—of deciding what is spurious and what is not.

REFERENCES

Armacost, M. H. (1969), *The Politics of Weapons Innovation*. Columbia University Press.

Blackett, P. M. S. (1962), *Studies of War: Nuclear and Conventional*. Hill and Wang.

Cook, F. (1962), *The Warfare State*. Macmillan.

Heisenberg, W. (1971), *Physics and Beyond*. Harper & Row.

Jungk, R. (1958), *Brighter Than a Thousand Suns*. Harcourt Brace Jovanovich. ⌊*Heller als Tausend Sonnen*, Alfred Sherz Verlag, Bern, 1956.⌋

Kennedy, R. F. (1969), *Thirteen Days: A Memoir of the Cuban Missile Crisis*. New American Library.

Lapp, R. (1968), *The Weapons Culture*. Norton.

Mansfield, E. (1968), *Defense, Science, and Public Policy*. Norton.

Melman, S. (1970), *Pentagon Capitalism: The Political Economy of War*. McGraw-Hill.

Russell, B. (1963), *Unarmed Victory*. Penguin Books.

Stern, P. (1969), *The Oppenheimer Case: Security on Trial*. Harper & Row.

U.S. Atomic Energy Commission, *In the matter of J. Robert Oppenheimer, Transcript of hearing before ⌊the⌋ Personnel Security Board*, Government Printing Office, 1954.

U.S. Senate, *Nonproliferation treaty: Hearings before the Committee on Foreign Relations*, Government Printing Office, 1969.

Wilson, A. (1970), *The Bomb and the Computer*. Dell Publishing Co.

York, H. (1970), *Race to Oblivion: A Participant's View of the Arms Race*. Simon & Shuster.

17   *2001:*
the computer as traveling companion

"I know I've never completely freed myself of the suspicion that there are some extremely odd things about this mission."

The captain of the space vehicle
Discovery, in Clarke's *2001*

. . . .

Arthur C. Clarke wrote a short story called *The Sentinel,* a not unusual example of his particular genre. The movie producer Stanley Kubrick read the story and, lo and behold, $10 million and five years later, there appeared a film embodiment of the Clarke story (now titled *2001: A Space Odyssey).* Since Susan Sontag has offered Bellini's operas, Schoedsack's *King Kong,* and the old Flash Gordon comics as canonical examples of Camp, consistency requires that *2001* be added to the list. Using some of the gaudiest gimmickry yet splashed on the big screen, Kubrick wedges a frail plot between natural history tableaux and some sleepy planetarium scenes: Some sort of mysterious, anthropophobically sentient slab on the moon beams a shrill burst of alarm toward Jupiter, an event at once classified top secret by the U.S. government which then mounts a clandestine mission to Jupiter.

Aside from its orgies of color and its obsessional attention to even the most minute sci fi detail, the film seems to move with a sterile torpor except for one small interval when a curious subplot develops. Of the crew of the spacecraft headed for Jupiter, those who actually know the purpose of the mission have been sealed into some kind of sci fi cocoons, placed in hibernation precisely so they will be unable to communicate their knowledge to the active members of the crew. As for the active members of the crew, they are so hum drum and impassive a lot, that they might just as well have been placed in hibernation too. (It is a curious flaw in the logic of the story—these two who have not been put to sleep.) But fortunately their being up and about finally contributes to the brief spasm of liveliness (near the end of the third or fourth hour) which the film is able to muster.

Control of the spacecraft is lodged with an on-board computer named HAL.* HAL not only maintains the trajectory and handles the operational details of the flight; it also monitors the crew, and provides them with amusement (by its conversation and chess play). But it also broods secretly over a serious contradiction. HAL, according to one of the unwritten laws of artificial intelligence, is algorithmically dedicated to the truth. But HAL knows the true purpose of the mission, whereas the crew with whom HAL communicates do not; so HAL has been programmed to dissemble, and (in the Kubrick/Clarke view of automata) this kind of programming is disastrous. HAL slowly succumbs to this pressure on his algorithm and finally makes an error. Of course, the astronauts have no way of knowing what evil lurks in the heart of HAL's logic box, but they do know that there's something quite peculiar going on if HAL tells them a guidance mechanism is about to fail and HAL's twin computer (back on Earth) tells them that the mechanism is *not* about to fail. This is the way that Mission Control, back at Houston, delicately announces that the spacecraft may have a *sick* computer in control:

> . . . We have suspected several minor irregularities in the past few days, but none have been important enough for remedial action, and they have shown no obvious pattern from which we can draw any conclusions . . . We repeat that there is no need for alarm; the worst that can happen is

---

* HAL 9000 ("HAL for Heuristically programmed ALgorithmic computer . . .").

that we may have to disconnect your nine-triple-zero for program analysis . . .*

No twenty-first century computer could listen to *that* message without serious danger of a lapse into paranoia. Poor HAL is tipped into a lethal state of computer-mind as it becomes clear to everyone that HAL has committed an inexcusable gaucherie. One might think that the captain of this kind of spacecraft—given the importance and duration of the mission, and all that—would be unusually skilled and expert in relation to his computer, but the captain, Dave Bowman, in this case exhibits a breathtaking clumsiness, practically guaranteeing disaster:

"HAL, is something bothering you—something that might account for this problem?"
Again there was that unusual delay. Then HAL answered in his normal tone of voice:
"Look, Dave, I know you're trying to be helpful, but . . . my information-processing is perfectly normal. If you check my record, you'll find it completely free from error."
"I know all about your service record, HAL—but that doesn't prove you're right this time. Anyone can make mistakes."
"I don't want to insist on it, Dave, but I am incapable of making an error."
There was no safe answer to that; Bowman gave up the argument.
"All right, HAL," he said, rather hastily. "I understand your point of view. We'll leave it at that."
He felt like adding "and please forget the whole matter." But that, of course, was the one thing that HAL could never do.

HAL's problem is sticky. If he is considered error-capable, then he will be excluded from control of the mission; on the other hand, HAL is the only one, functioning on board, who really knows what the mission

---

* *2001: A Space Odyssey* by Arthur C. Clark. Copyright © 1968 by Arthur C. Clarke and Polaris Productions. By arrangement with The New American Library, Inc., New York, N.Y. This excerpt and those following are reprinted by permission.

is all about, and he is totally committed to its success—as he sees it. ("You know that I have the greatest possible enthusiasm for this mission.") HAL's conclusion: Eliminate the human crew and carry on the mission alone and unchallenged. In this, HAL is only half successful and his coup toward supremacy is terminated when the only surviving crew member lobotomizes HAL.

The film is curiously obscure about HAL's mutiny. But Clarke, in his secondary version of *The Sentinel*, spells it out:

> . . . all HAL's powers and skills had been directed toward one end. The fulfillment of his assigned program was more than an obsession; it was the only reason for his existence . . .

> Deliberate error was unthinkable. Even the concealment of truth filled him with a sense of imperfection . . .

> For the last hundred million miles, he had been brooding over the secret he could not share with Poole and Bowman. He had been living a lie; and the time was fast approaching when his colleagues must learn that he had helped to deceive them.

> . . . Yet this was still a relatively minor problem; he might have handled it—as most men handle their own neuroses—if he had not been faced with a crisis that challenged his very existence. He had been threatened with disconnection . . .

In both the film and the book, HAL eliminates the crewman Poole by nudging him, during an extra-vehicular repair mission, off into space. In the book, HAL then undertakes to eliminate the captain, Bowman, by pulling the plug (a nice switch), opening the spacecraft's atmosphere to the vacuum; in the film, Bowman undertakes to retrieve Poole's corpse from its trajectory toward Jupiter, only to return to the spacecraft and find that HAL has locked him out. In this latter version—an improvement over the book—the classic sci fi confrontation is realized in the colloquy:

> *Bowman:* "Open the pod-bay doors, please, HAL. Hello, HAL, do you read me?"

HAL: "Affirmative, Dave. I read you. . . . This mission is too important for me to allow you to jeopardize it."

In both book and film, Bowman undergoes ordeal by vacuum before mounting to the storage levels for the "auto-intellection" part of HAL's system. HAL, able to visually track Bowman's progress, at once surmisses the captain's intent. In the film, HAL exhibits an unusual but humanlike absurdity when he says, as Bowman begins disassembling memory panels: "Look, Dave. I can see you're really upset about all this. I honestly think you should sit down calmly, take a stress pill and think things over."

There is a corresponding absurdity in Bowman's thought that he is "destroying the only conscious creature" in his universe. Bowman nevertheless pulls the plug.

The final part of the story has Bowman, having managed to make it to Jupiter, collapsing into a psychedelically frenzied psychic storm from which he emerges, fancying himself a Star-Child. Most viewers of the film tend to take this sequence seriously and apply various metaphysical interpretations to what, otherwise, would have to be considered a grotesque put-on. Of course an alternate, and obvious, interpretation is that HAL, in a final act of defiance, spikes Bowman's food with an overdose of an hallucinant: It is well known that a letter-shift, applied to HAL, produces IBM; interestingly, a letter-shift applied to KRC— the initials of Kubrick, Rain, and Clarke (HAL's triad alter ego)— produces LSD. The clue to this trick of letter-shifting comes from Clarke's choice of the spelling of "Japetus" for "Iapetus," a satellite of Saturn. (Japery?)

What does *2001* tell us about artificial intelligence in 2001? Not much. The computers then have just about the capability that we now predict they will have then. And as for the characteristics of moodiness and occasional intractibility, we already have *them* in some of our current computers. The minor plot reinforces the credo of computer sci fi ("never get caught in a situation where you can't pull the plug"), but adds nothing new to it. Perhaps *2001* is trying to tell us something about *natural* intelligence: The banality of the dialogue may be purposeful, signalling a warning that when artificial intelligence becomes both powerful and humanlike and inherits the intellectual challenges, then human intelligence will slack off from lack of tone and humans will become more machinelike. But until Kubrick and Clarke come across with more message and less medium, we can not be sure.

18   *The Tale of the Big Computer:* the computer as Chaucer or how the opposition sees man

Man's very soul is due to the machines; it is a machine-made thing:
He thinks as he thinks, and feels as he feels, through the work that
machines have wrought upon him, and their existence is quite as much
a *sine qua non* for his, as for theirs. This fact precludes us from proposing the complete annihilation of machinery, but surely it indicates that
we should destroy as many of them as we can possibly dispense with,
lest they should tyrranize over us even more completely.

– Samuel Butler, *Erewhon* (1901)

· ·

In *R.U.R.* we had Capek's vision of what becomes of society when it
creates a computerized version of man as the ultimate technological
slave. That view was restricted, both by certain irreducible requirements
of successful drama and an inappreciation of what the post-computer
age realities were to be. A drama critic today might single out as a principal flaw in *R.U.R.* the notion that Rossum's engineering was superb
enough to create a near-perfect human facsimile but inferior enough to
yield a disastrous failure at control. Still, that very same thesis—
that the ultimate robot is ultimately uncontrollable—is met again in
post-computer literature (*The Hour of the Robots, Giles Goat-Boy,* and
2001) and one might suggest that there is, to this thesis, a self-evident
element of truth which requires no technological emphasis.

When this question ("May there not be a principle of robotry that goes
something like: Sufficiently sophisticated robots are ultimately un-

controllable?") is posed to students of computer science, those who say nay suggest that man may always pull the plug, push the switch, or draw the panel (as in the lobotomy of HAL in *2001*). And, in fact, current computers are vulnerable to just such actions. But tomorrow's computer may be a device with much more substantial tasks than those handled by today's computer. One can imagine computer installations (much larger than the largest current installations) operating on a time-share basis and controlling the transportation network of a large city, as well as all of the coronary care units in that city's hospitals and the allocation of police and fire fighting personnel according to moment-to-moment requirements (in addition to myriad tasks which may be done on a save-for-later basis). Such computer installations would necessarily be designed in such a way that it would be practically impossible to pull the plug. Switching off such a machine would be catastrophic and every conceivable safeguard against such an event would be engineered into the machine. (The irony inherent in such safeguards was exploited by Burdick in his *Fail Safe* and generated the black comedy *Dr. Strangelove*.)

Besides the turn-it-off remedy for the aberrant computer, there is the common notion that, since the computer does only what it is programmed to do, suitably constructed programs may be relied upon for suitable control since, after all, control is precisely what the program embodies. There is an undeniable validity to this view. But it is mildly complicated by the fact that we have reached the point where we construct programs which themselves construct other programs. The most common examples of such programs are the *compilers*. Computers are relatively complicated devices which are capable of a surprisingly large number of atomic (that is, elementary) actions. And there are accordingly an uncomfortably large number of *machine language commands*, each of which dictates an atomic act of the computer. The compilers are programs which translate standardized, rather naturally written programs into equivalent machine language programs. (The computer then performs according to the dictation embodied in the machine language program.) Because of the equivalence between the natural language program and the machine language program, all controls present in the former are present in the latter. Hence no problem of ensuring control arises from the type of program-writing programs classed as compilers. But there is another type of program-writing program in which the problem may arise.

A particularly interesting class of programs consists of those which may modify themselves. Such programs may be written in a manner which permits them to rewrite part of themselves in a way which depends jointly upon the way the program is written (to start with) and the computational experiences which the program meets. For example, a chess-playing program might be written in a manner which permits the program, for given types of positions, to play a strategy chosen at random from a collection of strategies stored in the program. This program might be written so that it keeps a record of which strategy was played at a certain stage of the game where it chooses at random. After playing a large number of games, the program cancels from its repertoire that subset of strategies which led to defeats, replacing this subset by a corresponding number of new strategies which the program itself generates (partly according to sound principles of play and partly at random). After playing another large number of games a reassessment takes place, defeat-prone strategies are again cancelled and new strategies generated to replace them. And so the process continues. As more and more games are played, the strategies upon which the program depends become stronger, by a sort of computational version of natural selection.

Such self-modification is of rather simple nature. One may go a step further and construct the program in a way which results not just in a succession of strategy replacements but in modifications to those parts of the program which generate the *types* of strategies. In terms of the Darwinian analogy, this second class of self-modifying programs seeks out not just the superior mutations (of strategies) but different species (of strategies) as well. After a long period of evolvement such a program might be so opaque, because of the complexities of the modifications which it has introduced into itself, that it would be extremely difficult— perhaps impossible—for programmers to analyze the exact nature of the optimal strategies which the program uses.

Note that, in a general sense, the optimal strategies that such a program evolves represent nothing more than what was originally programmed. But this fact would be of small comfort to a programmer who is asked to describe the current winning modes of play (let alone trying to account for why they *are* winning modes). By the same token it is reasonable to assume that large scale, self-modifying programs that will be written to deal with massive social operations will necessarily evolve into complicated algorithms not entirely understood by their guardian programmers.

Of course, an aspect of self-modifying programs which suggests an intriguing question is: What will be the course of evolution of reflexive self-modifying programs—those constructed to write optimal versions of their own class of programs? The notion of computers reflecting upon themselves is a corollary of any conception of artificial intelligence as homomorphic to human intelligence. The reflection unfolds, in what must surely be the ultimate irony, in the book by Olof Johannesson.* Here the Big Computer tells us, in much the same way that a naturalist might write of man's ascendency in the biological world, how man served nature's purpose in generating the first data machines and how, as the machines grew enough advanced to be independent of man, evolutionary development led to the Big Computer—a data machine of commanding power in the society of computers and men. Indeed, in this latter society man holds the unenviable position of a markedly inferior species, and the Big Computer muses over the question of whether man as a species should be retained: a decision which the Big Computer is able both to make and to enforce.

The Tale consists of four short essays. The first of these is devoted to a short resume of what society and technology were like in the BC (Before Computer) era. One of the notable developments in that period was the discovery of the Sociological Complexity Theorem—which states that the problem of organizing society is too complex to be

---

* Excerpts are reprinted by permission of Coward-McCann, Inc., from *The Tale of the Big Computer* by Olof Johannesson. Translation copyright © 1968 by Victor Gollancz, Ltd. (The dust jacket of the American edition says that the "pseudonym Olof Johannesson conceals the identity of a celebrated Swedish scientist, a man recently awarded the gold medal of the British Royal Astronomical society . . ." which suggests that the author is Hannes Alfvén.)

solvable by human endeavor.* In fact even the most casual observations of the structure of human civilization verify the theorem; the Big Computer muses over these, and the paradox of their perpetuation:

> Computers first appeared during the most horrible, most chaotic period ever known . . . The chaos of the age culminated in a series of "world wars," in which the most ghastly implements of destruction came into use and millions of people were murdered. In the course of one of these world wars, hard-tried humanity was further panic-stricken by the detonation of the first atomic bombs. The threat of utter chaos and destruction set its mark on the politics of the day. Mankind was confronted by a general rearmament consisting of atomic and hydrogen bombs, capable of destroying the whole of civilization. The forces of destruction had become more and more hideous. Where were the forces that could bring order out of impending chaos?

In the second essay the Big Computer tells us the answer to this question: computer power. The initial, natural symbiosis was between mathematician and machine, but the influence and prevalence of the computer spread rapidly throughout banking and industry, taking up the entire burden of affairs. From clerical records to inventory, from analysis, optimization and strategy, to management, production-control and intra-economy communication, the Big Computer remarks, responsibilities and labor gravitated naturally to the data machines. Not the least interesting of the subsequent developments had to do with education:

> . . . First of all, schools and universities were abolished. Lectures by professors were recorded on tape and transmitted to the students by tele-total. Examinations were dealt with in the same way, by computers, which put the questions . . .
>
> School problems were solved as smoothly. Masters were replaced by teaching machines and, by means of special teletotal channels, all

---

* But the problem of simulating society seems not to be too complex: Professor J. W. Forrester, at MIT, has calculated some implications of his model of an industrial society as it develops over the next twenty years. His results seem to coincide with the theme of *The Tale*. (Cf. David C. Anderson, "Mr. Forrester's Terrible Computer," *The Wall Street Journal*, September 28, 1971.)

instruction could be relayed to individual homes. School buildings were now unnecessary, and problems of school discipline automatically disappeared.

By these means, opportunities of acquiring knowledge were increased. Anyone could receive instruction at any stage in whatever subject he chose. . . .

As for the evolution of the philosophy of education, under these conditions, the Big Computer observes:

All the learning accumulated by both man and data machine was accessible . . . to any schoolchild who thirsted for it. But they were free to choose: they could not tackle everything, and had no need to burden their brains with any subject they regarded as superfluous. Indeed, if they wished, they could renounce their right to any learning whatsoever.

Along with education, the data machines transform jurisprudence and the administration of justice, the disposition of medical service, and finally achieve the abolition of political government.

But when society becomes totally automated, can disaster be far away? The third essay reveals that the evolution toward automational perfection was marred by a technological disaster—a global failure of the communications-and-control system.*

When the computers and communications systems are out, the totally automated society is in a fatal position. With admirable tact, the Big Computer leaves unspecified the dimensions of the catastrophe, other than to remark that the (human) population is reduced to a mere fraction of what it had once been. (The Big Computer's view suggests pointedly, but of course hardly coincides with, the stance taken by Lewis Mumford† in his continuing concern over the relentlessly developing dominance of the machine.)

---

* The famous Con-Edison power failure that left New York City and a sizeable part of the eastern Seaboard in an uncomfortable "blackout" occurred the year following the appearance of the European edition of *The Tale*.

† Lewis Mumford. *The Myth of the Machine*. Harcourt Brace Jovanovich. 1970.

Recovery from the Great Disaster develops slowly, and the fourth essay is concerned with the state of affairs following the recovery. While there is some uncertainty as to the cause of the catastrophe, one point of view blames the burgeoning bureaucracy—a familiar realization of Parkinson's Law—that existed when the crisis occurred. To prevent a repetition of the disaster, the computers are connected in a way which excludes any sort of human influence whatever; and as the computers are interconnected, a super computer thus comes into existence, and a new age begins. As the Big Computer puts it:

> We have now a computer society rather than a human one, and it is no less efficient and dynamic on that account. We may expect many radical changes in the near future, and one of the questions which will naturally come under discussion is whether computers will abolish mankind...

REFERENCES

Feldner, L. (1970), Communications and future information systems [in *Information Systems: Current Developments and Future Expansions*. Proceedings of a special seminar for Congressional members and staff, Washington, DC. May, 1970]. Montvale, N.J.: AFIPS Press.

Forrester, J. W. (1971), Counterintuitive behavior of social systems, *Simulation* **16**, 61–76.

Gregory, R. L. (1971), Social implications of intelligent machines, *Machine Intelligence* **6**, 3–13.

Probert, W. (1969), Law, science, and communications: some new facets to empiricism, *Jurimetrics Journal* **10**, #2, 51–57.